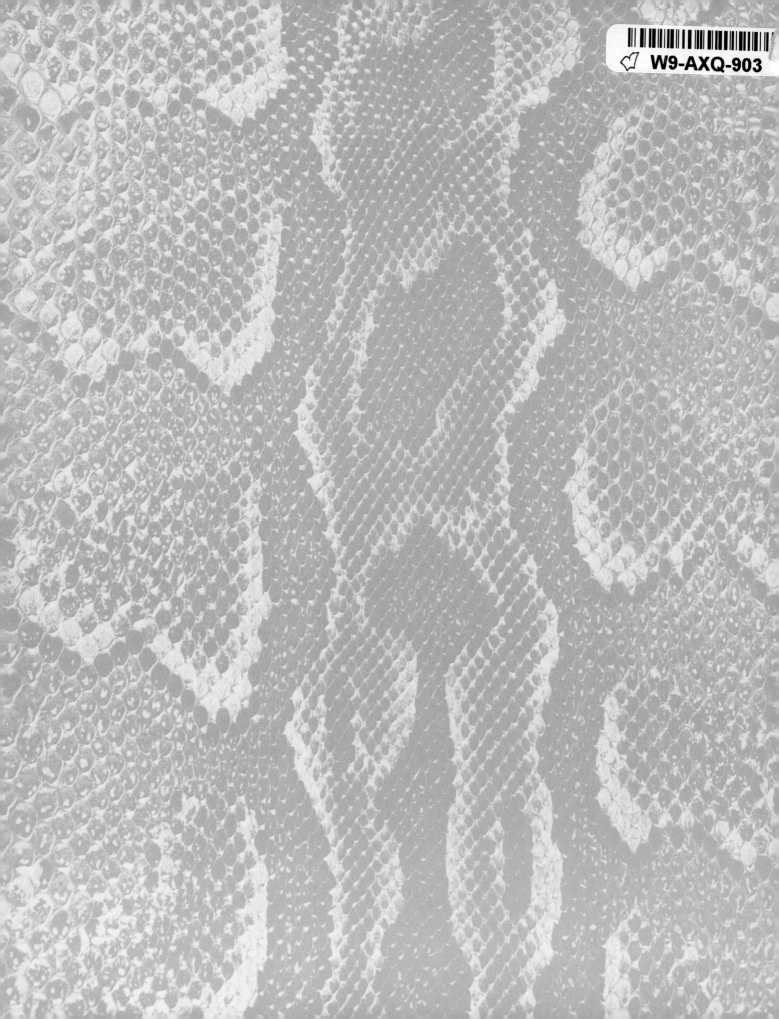

SNAKES

SNAKES

A concise guide to nature's perfect predators

Daniel Gilpin

Parragon

Bath · New York · Singapore · Hong Kong · Cologne · Delhi · Melbourne

First published by Parragon in 2007
Parragon
Queen Street House
4 Queen Street
Bath BA1 1HE, UK

Designed, produced and packaged by
Stonecastle Graphics Limited

Text by Daniel Gilpin
Edited by Anthony John
Designed by Sue Pressley and Paul Turner

ISBN 978-1-4075-0193-2

Printed in Dubai

CONTENTS

THE SNAKE 6

What is a Snake? 8
Types of Snake 14

SNAKE BEHAVIOR 20

Senses and Movement 22
Predators and Prey 34
Breeding and Young 44

SNAKE FAMILIES 50

Venomous Snakes 52
Constrictors 64
Other Snakes 76

SNAKE FACTS 86

Snake Snippets 88
Snake Directory 90

INDEX 96

THE SNAKE

Snakes have a powerful hold over the
human imagination. The first reaction most
people have when they encounter one is fear.
As with most fears, the fear of snakes –
ophiophobia – can be conquered by knowledge.
The more we learn about these creatures the
more fascinating they become. Snakes are
highly evolved predators perfectly adapted for
the lives that they lead. Some hunt in trees,
some on the ground, and others in the sea.
The vast majority are completely harmless to
humans. Even those that are dangerous hardly
ever attack unless provoked.

WHAT IS A SNAKE?

Most people would recognize a snake if they saw one. Snakes are legless reptiles that swallow their food whole. Like all reptiles, they have dry, scaly skin, which they shed periodically as they grow.

There are more than 2500 different species of snake known to science. Every single one of them, without exception, is carnivorous and all but a few egg-eating specialists hunt living animals. Unlike crocodilians and some lizards, snakes avoid carrion: they only eat what they have captured and killed themselves.

Snakes are cold-blooded animals, which means that their internal body temperature changes with that of their surroundings. In tropical regions, where it is continually warm, they are active all year round, day and night, but elsewhere their behavior changes with the time of day and the seasons. In order to warm their bodies up enough to enable them to become active, they bask in the morning sun. At night and during the colder months they seek shelter and become sluggish. This dependence on warm surroundings restricts where they can live.

There are no snakes north of the Arctic Circle and they are absent from large parts of Canada. They are also absent from the higher parts of most mountain chains, particularly those far away from the Equator. (The snake found at the highest altitudes is the Himalayan Pit Viper *(Agkistrodon himalayanus)*, which occurs 16076ft (4900m) above sea level).

At the limits of their natural range, snakes spend the winter in hibernation. As summer turns to fall, they seek out natural crevices, caverns and the burrows of other animals, where the worst of the frosts cannot reach. They then curl up in preparation for the cold months ahead. The most suitable sites are often shared by several individuals and sometimes snakes of different species hibernate together. As the temperature drops, each snake's heartbeat slows until it is barely ticking over and the amount of energy used by its body decreases many times.

Snake classification

Snakes are classified by scientists into the same order of reptiles as lizards, the order Squamata. Within that order, snakes have their own suborder, Serpentes. Like lizards, snakes have special bones in their skulls, the quadrate bones, which enable them to move their upper jaws relative to the braincase. This gives their jaws much greater flexibility than those of other reptiles and also makes their bites much

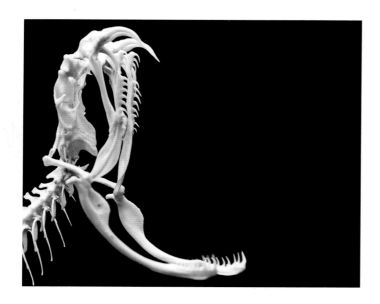

more powerful for their size than they would otherwise be. Added to this, snakes have the ability to completely dislocate their lower jaws, which allows them to swallow prey with bodies much wider than their own. This ability and the fact that the two halves of their lower jaws are not rigidly attached is what separates them from lizards.

Many people wrongly assume that the feature that separates snakes from lizards is the absence of legs. In fact, there are many species of legless lizard, including the slow-worm *(Anguis fragilis)*, which is native to Europe. The amphisbaenians, a group of legless burrowing lizards common in South America and Africa, actually have their own suborder, like snakes.

Above: *Snakes can open their mouths incredibly wide and they can also unhinge their jaws. The lower jaws can also be moved apart from one another. In life, they are connected at the front by an elastic ligament. This is the skull of a Western Diamondback Rattlesnake (Crotalus atrox), with its large front fangs ready to strike.*

Opposite: *Snakes are incredibly flexible. Their many vertebrae and ribs are connected by literally hundreds of different muscles which enable them to contort their bodies into virtually any shape. This flexibility allows snakes to move with ease through most types of terrain, and follow their prey almost anywhere.*

Below: *Lacking limbs, snakes have the simplest skeletons of any vertebrates, consisting of just a skull, a backbone and numerous ribs. Pythons and some other primitive snakes show vestiges of pelvic bones but in the majority of snakes, such as this Gaboon Viper (Bitis gabonica), these have been lost completely.*

Previous pages: *The slow-worm (Anguis fragilis, left) is not a snake but, rather, a legless lizard. Its jaws are not flexible but fixed, a feature that separates lizards from snakes. Unlike the slow-worm, the Green Rat Snake (Senticolis triaspis intermedia, right) from the south-western USA and Central America is able to swallow prey much wider than itself.*

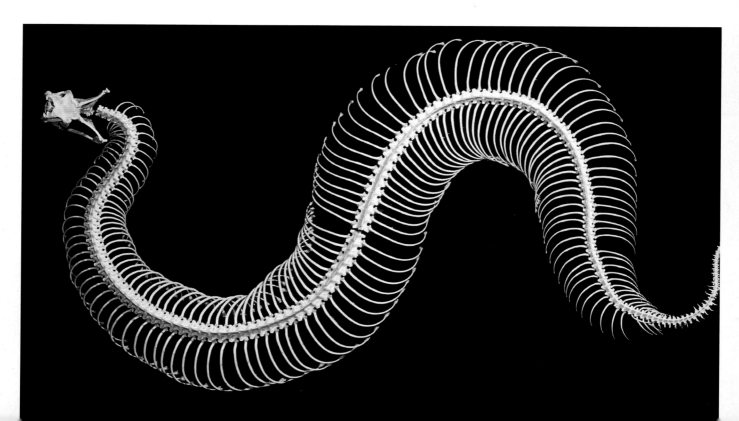

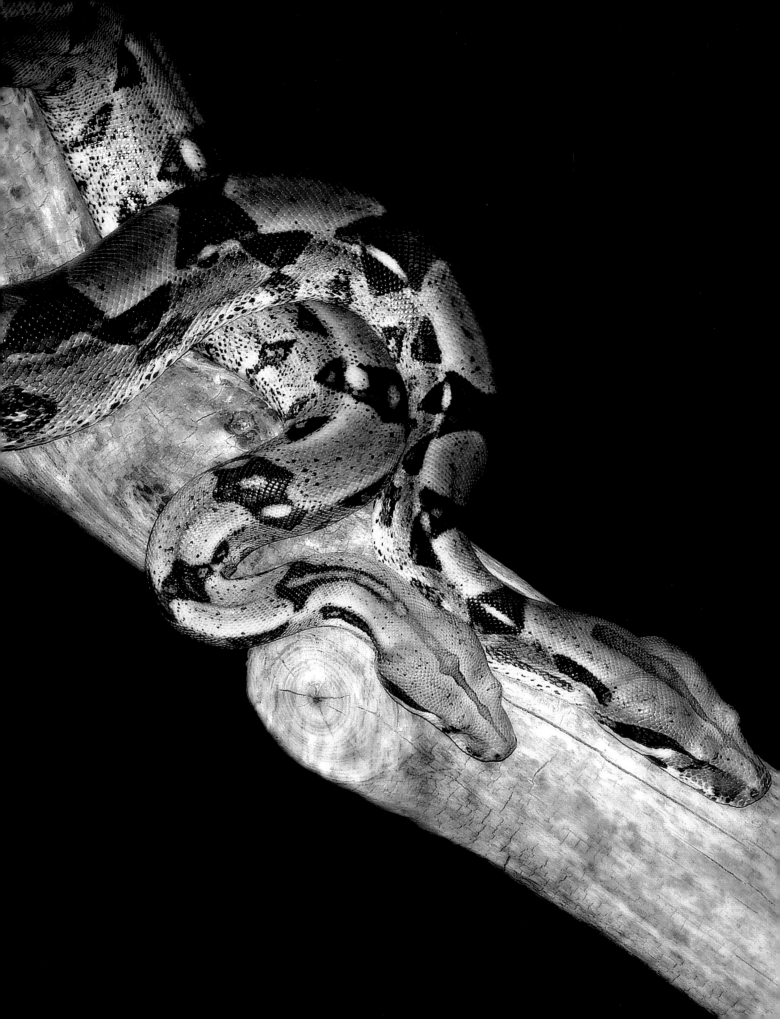

Skin and bones

The skin of snakes is covered by thousands of scales. Each of these is individually colored and in many species they are grouped to form quite beautiful patterns. Generally speaking, snakes are colored and patterned for camouflage, enabling them to lie in wait hidden from prey or creep slowly and unseen toward it. Some snakes, however, are so brightly colored and boldly patterned that they can be seen from some way off. These species tend to be venomous and their outfits act like warning flags, telling other, larger, predators to leave them alone.

Besides determining a snake's color, the scales serve to protect its body from abrasion and damage. Those on the back and sides of the body tend to be smaller and thinner than those underneath. The large belly scales form the points of contact between the muscles used in locomotion and the ground.

Snakes, like other reptiles, continue to grow throughout life but their scales, once formed, are fixed in size. It is for this reason that these animals shed their skin. Most species shed the whole of their skin in one go, leaving a delicate, cast-off replica of their former selves, known as a slough. Just before this process begins, most snakes take on a bluish hue and their eyes go cloudy. This is caused by the build-up of fluid between the old and new layers of skin.

The skeletons of snakes are among the simplest of those of any vertebrates. Most consist of just vertebrae, ribs, and a skull. Boas and pythons retain the vestiges of hind limbs – a clue to the fact that snakes evolved from reptiles with legs. These greatly reduced pelvic bones break the surface as tiny spurs in some species. The bones of a snake's skeleton form the anchor points for its muscles. These perform two functions, locomotion and the movement of swallowed prey through the digestive system.

Above: Unlike mammals, which lose and replace tiny sections of their skin every day as dust, snakes shed their entire skins at once. This process is known as sloughing and happens every few months throughout a snake's life.

Top: The scales on a snake's belly tend to be larger than those on its upper side and often stretch right across the body. Their size and shape helps the snake to grip the surface over which it is moving.

Left: Many snakes, such as these Boa Constrictors (Boa constrictor), have beautifully patterned skin. Patterns may serve to camouflage snakes or act as warning signals, advertising the fact that they are dangerous to potential predators.

TYPES OF SNAKE

Snakes can be divided up in a number of ways. Most people would automatically split them into venomous and non-venomous species but they can also be grouped by other physical characteristics.

Scientists divide the 2500 or so species of snake into three main groups known as superfamilies. The first of these superfamilies, Henophidia, contains the boas, pythons, and other primitive snakes. The second, Typhlopoidea, contains the tiny blind snakes and threadsnakes and the third, Xenophidia, contains all other snakes. The three superfamilies are further subdivided into families. There are 19 different snake families in all.

By far the largest of these families is the family Colubridae, which contains more than half of all the snake species on Earth. Colubrids are characterized by their broad belly scales, which usually stretch the entire width of the body, their cylindrical, pointed tails and their generally oval-shaped heads. Most species are harmless and the few that do produce venom, such as the Boomslang *(Dispholidus typus),* inject it using fangs at the back of the mouth.

The vast majority of the world's venomous snakes belong to one of two families, the Viperidae and the Elapidae. The family Viperidae contains all of the vipers, including the pit vipers. There are 224 species in this family, among them the common European adder *(Vipera berus)* found throughout most of Eurasia. The family Elapidae contains the cobras and their relatives, which include all of Australia's venomous snakes. Both vipers and elapids have long fangs at the front of their mouths which they use to inject venom.

Blind snakes and threadsnakes make up three families, separated mainly by their internal anatomy. These tiny snakes look not unlike earthworms and some are little bigger than those invertebrates. Most of the 360 or so species feed on the larvae of termites and ants. Because of their small size and burrowing habits, blind snakes and threadsnakes are still quite poorly understood.

Pythons and boas, on the other hand, are both well known and well studied. These snakes, which kill their prey by constriction, make up two families, the Pythonidae and the Boidae, and include the largest snakes in the world.

Pythons and boas are often confused in the public imagination and the two groups do share a great many similarities. The main difference between them anatomically is that pythons have teeth on the premaxilla (the bone that makes up the very front part of the skull and upper jaw) while boas do not. Pythons and boas are also separated

geographically. Boas are confined to Central and South America, Madagascar, Fiji, and the Solomon Islands. Pythons are absent from all these places, but are found throughout much of mainland Africa, southern Asia, and Australia.

Close families

The other major snake family is the family Hydrophiidae, which contains the sea snakes. Sea snakes are closely related to cobras and some scientists classify them as elapids rather than giving them a family of their own. Sea snakes differ from their land-living cousins in a number of respects, most notably their body shape which is flattened toward the tail as an adaptation for swimming. They also have much smaller heads for their size than most other snakes. Altogether there are around 50 species of sea snake known to science. All of them are venomous, with relatively short fangs located near the front of the upper jaw.

The other snake families are all small with most containing fewer than 10 species. Among them is the family Acrochordidae, which contains the bizarre-looking wart snakes. These entirely aquatic, fish-eating snakes live in the rivers, streams, and estuaries of South-East Asia and Australia. All have very simple scales and extremely loose-fitting skin, which looks a couple of sizes too big for them. Although they are entirely harmless to humans, wart snakes are thick-bodied and the largest, the Elephant's Trunk Snake (*Acrochordus javanicus*), can grow to well over 6ft 7in (2m) long.

Above: With its telltale oval head, the Common Garter Snake (Thamnophis sirtalis) from North America is a typical colubrid. Colubrids make up the majority of snake species on Earth.

Previous pages: Boas (left) have almost triangular heads, which bulge behind the temples. Unlike other elapids, cobras (right) have a hood which they raise when they feel threatened.

Following pages: The Rough-scaled Bush Viper (Atheris squamiger) is one of the world's smaller vipers, rarely growing to more than 2ft 6in (75cm) long. It lives in tropical West and Central Africa and spends most of its life up in the branches.

SNAKE BEHAVIOR

Like most animals, snakes are driven by
two main urges, the urge to feed and the urge
to reproduce. These urges lie behind most of
their behavior. A snake's hunting strategy is an
evolutionary response to satisfy hunger and avoid
starvation. Snakes invariably hunt alone but the
methods they employ to capture prey differ.
Attracting a mate or seeking one out is a
response to the urge to reproduce, an instinctive
drive to pass on genes to the next generation.
Snake behavior is driven by instinct but it is
enabled by their senses and their ability
to get around.

SENSES AND MOVEMENT

Snakes see the world somewhat differently from us. Their color vision, while not poor, is more limited than ours, and they tend to have difficulty distinguishing from the background objects that are not moving. A yellow filter in the lens protects their eyes from ultraviolet light and they have rod cells in their retinas, as we do, which can tell the difference between subtle shades of light and dark. Rod cells are more numerous in the eyes of nocturnal snakes: color-detecting cone cells do not work in the low light levels after dusk.

Although some snakes depend on their eyes to locate prey and find their way around – particularly arboreal species that are active by day – vision is not the primary sense for most of these reptiles. Snakes are creatures that follow their noses or, more accurately, their tongues.

The fact that snakes have forked tongues is one of the first things we learn about them as children. What few of us are ever told is why. Snakes use their tongues in the same way as mammals use their nostrils – to pick up scent particles from the air. The continual flicking in and out is rather like the repeated sniffing actions a dog makes – with each flick the snake is picking up more information. As the snake withdraws its tongue, the two tips enter grooves in the roof of the mouth and deposit the particles it has picked up on to sensitive patches of an organ known as the Jacobson's organ. The brain then analyzes the information that has been deposited there. If more particles of a particular scent were deposited by the left fork of the tongue than the right, then the snake knows that whatever released those particles is to its left. When the number of those particles deposited by each fork is roughly the same, then the snake knows its head is pointed directly toward it.

Snakes use this sense to help them track down prey that is out of sight. (They also use this sense to detect potential mates and follow other snakes to hibernation dens in winter.) Once they are in visual range, however, their eyesight takes over, following the movements of the targeted prey until they are ready to strike.

Of course, not all snakes hunt in the daylight. Many species in the warmer parts of the world are more active as predators after dusk. Vision plays a part for these snakes when they hunt on moonlit nights but most nocturnal snakes rely on another sense, the ability to detect heat. Heat detection is a specialty of the pythons, boas, pit vipers, rattlesnakes and their relatives. All of these snakes have specialized organs located on the front of the head that are

extremely sensitive to subtle differences in temperature. Pit vipers and rattlesnakes have two of these organs, one on each side of the head between the eye and the tip of the snout. Pythons and boas, on the other hand, have several, located along the upper lip. These heat-detecting organs are so sensitive that snakes can actually use them to 'see' their prey in complete darkness. The body heat given off by animals forms an image of their outline, much like that detected by an infrared camera, and the snakes are able to target this and strike just as easily as if they were looking at the animals by day.

While some snakes have this extra sense that we do not, they lack something that we take for granted – external ears. As a result, their sense of hearing is extremely reduced. Sound vibrations are transmitted to their internal ears through the lower jaws. While they can detect loud thuds, most of the world must sound extremely muffled to them, much as it does to us when we stick our fingers in our ears. The myth of the cobra dancing to the snake charmer's music is just that. Rather, the snake simply responds to the movement of the charmer and his pipe.

Above right: *Pythons have heat-sensing pits in the scales of their upper lip, just beneath the nostrils. These help them to locate their prey at night, enabling them to strike in darkness when they themselves cannot be seen.*

Right: *A snake's sense of hearing is virtually non-existent. Snakes lack external ears but can detect vibrations through the ground.*

Opposite: *Vision is an important sense, particularly to tree-climbing snakes. These species tend to have larger eyes than most other snakes.*

Previous pages: *A Red-tailed Rat Snake (Gonyosoma oxycephala) opens its mouth, showing the pit in the roof that contains the Jacobson's organ. Snakes use their forked tongues to taste the air (right) then transfer particles from the tips into the organ where they are analyzed.*

Following pages: *Rattlesnakes have heat-sensing organs in pits between the eyes and mouth. The tongue flickers in and out continuously – passing through a hole which is always open, even when the mouth is closed.*

Getting around

One might imagine that having no legs might restrict a snake's ability to get around but in fact nothing could be further from the truth. Snakes have evolved the ability not only to slither but also to burrow, climb, swim, and even glide.

Most of the world's snakes live on the ground and slither along using serpentine movement, creating S-shapes with their bodies. This form of locomotion is extremely efficient and enables snakes to move quite quickly. As the snake moves, its body undulates from side to side with just the outer edge of each curve making contact with the ground. The edge of the body grips and pushes against any irregularities on the surface, enabling the snake to drive its entire body forward.

A variation on this serpentine movement is used by desert snakes to travel over sand. Known as sidewinding, it has evolved at least twice in different parts of the world. In North America it is used by the Sidewinder Rattlesnake *(Crotalus cerastes)* and in Africa by the Horned Viper *(Cerastes cerastes)*, two snakes that are only distantly related but have evolved to survive in similar habitats. When sidewinding, much of the snake's body is actually in the air. With the outer edges of just two or three curves in its body touching the sand, it throws its head and the front part of its body sideways, at a right angle to the direction in which the next part of its body is facing. Sidewinding enables these snakes to both move quickly over the hot desert sand and minimize their contact with it.

Opposite: Sidewinders leave distinctive tracks in the sand as they move. These show how the snake throws the front of its body through the air and maintains only minimal contact with the hot surface.

Above: Snakes have incredibly flexible bodies and can virtually tie their bodies into knots. Most snakes move using serpentine movement, creating S-shapes to help them grip even the slightest irregularities in the surface.

Snakes that swim basically use serpentine movement underwater. Sea snakes have bodies that have adapted to make this movement more efficient, with tails that have become flattened like paddles. The world's largest snake, the Green Anaconda *(Eunectes murinus),* is another excellent swimmer and spends much of its time in the water. Large adults are too bulky to move very quickly on land, although younger individuals sometimes lurk in branches above tracks used by other animals, close enough to attack them as they walk beneath.

Serpentine movement is employed by all snakes at some time or another but large, heavy-bodied snakes tend to move in a different way. Unless startled, they shuffle slowly along in a straight line. This sort of locomotion, known as rectilinear locomotion, is achieved by rippling movements which run down the belly from head to tail. The large belly scales, which overlap like roof tiles, individually grip the ground with their edges to push the snake along gradually.

Above: *Sea snakes swim in much the same way as most snakes move on land. Rather than using their bodies to grip, however, they move by means of their flattened tails, which act like paddles.*

Right: *A snake's skeleton gives it flexibility and its muscles give it strength. This Children's Python* (Antaresia childreni) *has lifted the front part of its body up in a defensive posture and is ready to strike.*

Slow but sure

Occasionally snakes employ a third form of locomotion, known as concertina movement. With this system, the front part of the body is creased up into bends and the rear part pulled toward it. As the rear end of the snake is pulled forward, it too is creased up into tight bends. The front part is then stretched out, pushing the head forward and the whole process is repeated again. Concertina movement is slow but sure and often used by snakes when climbing to negotiate a smooth or slippery branch.

Most snakes are capable of climbing if necessary but some are adapted to spending most of their lives in the trees. Arboreal snakes tend to be either long and slender, or short and stubby. The former, such as the vine snakes, travel through the branches by serpentine movement, while the latter, which include the tree-living boas and pythons, use rectilinear locomotion and have prehensile tails, which they wrap around branches for safety. Many arboreal snakes also have strongly keeled belly scales which enable them to grip tightly the cracks and crevices in bark, some tightly enough to scale vertical tree trunks.

Five species of snake can actually travel through the air. Known as the flying snakes, they glide between trees in the rainforests of South-East Asia where they live, to escape predators and also to reach new trees without having to descend to the ground. Flying snakes catch the air by extending their ribs outward to flatten their bodies and move through it with a serpentine motion, as if swimming. This gives them some degree of control over the direction they take, enabling them to steer toward outstretched branches below.

Above right: *The Yellow Anaconda* (Eunectes notaeus) *is a close relative of the better known and gigantic Green Anaconda* (Eunectes murinus). *The Yellow Anaconda, like its cousin, spends much of its time in water.*

Right: *The Reticulated Python* (Python reticulatus) *is the world's longest snake and moves mainly by rectilinear locomotion, shuffling its huge body along. Compared with serpentine movement, rectilinear locomotion is relatively slow.*

Left: Tree-climbing snakes are incredibly good at distributing their weight evenly. Many are so small and light that they can balance on the tiniest twigs, allowing them to reach small prey out among the leaves.

Below: The majority of small arboreal snakes are green for camouflage. Their long, slender bodies enable them to stretch out and reach across many gaps between branches, meaning that in forests or thickets they rarely have to descend to the ground.

PREDATORS AND PREY

Snakes are almost unique in the animal kingdom in being able to swallow prey much larger than themselves. They achieve this impressive feat by having extremely flexible mouths, with lower jaws that unhinge from their skulls and stretch in the middle. The lower jaw bones are connected underneath by extremely strong but elastic ligaments. These enable the bones to move apart to accommodate large meals but pull them back together once the snake has swallowed.

Understandably, snakes swallow their prey very slowly and only once it has been killed or stopped struggling. Most prey is swallowed head first, to prevent legs, fins, or other appendages sticking in the throat. Snakes neither dismember nor chew their prey but swallow it whole. They do this by moving each side of the mouth independently. While the left lower jaw is held still, the right is moved slightly forward. This is then held in position while the left is moved forward a fraction. In this way, the snake slowly but surely 'walks' the prey into its mouth. Small meals may be swallowed in a matter of minutes but large animals may take two or three hours to go down.

Once a snake has closed its mouth on a meal, the process of getting it down to the stomach continues. This is done by rhythmic contractions of the muscles in the snake's body. The tube linking the mouth to the stomach, the esophagus, is relatively simple. In humans and other mammals, it is this tube that contracts to move food down, rather than the muscles around it.

Snakes take some time to digest their meals and this process, like all of a snake's bodily functions, slows down as the temperature drops. A large meal may last a snake in the tropics for two or three weeks. Over winter in colder climates, a snake may survive as long as six months between meals.

When it comes to selecting a meal, most snakes are opportunists, attacking whatever they encounter and they are big enough to kill and swallow. A few species, however, have become specialists. The African snakes of the genus *Dasypeltis* have evolved to live entirely on a diet of birds' eggs. As one might expect, these egg-eating snakes are expert climbers and spend much of their time in the branches seeking out birds' nests. When an egg-eating snake finds a meal, it swallows the egg whole, moving it into its esophagus and closing its mouth. With the egg swallowed, it uses bony projections in its throat to crack the shell and then crushes it. The contents are then moved down into the stomach and the indigestible fragments of eggshell are later regurgitated.

Specialist feeders

Other snakes specialize in hunting particular types of prey. The Siamese River Snake *(Herpeton tentaculatum)*, for example, feeds almost entirely on fish. On the end of its snout it has two fleshy tentacles which it wriggles to lure fish into striking range. Other adaptations to its aquatic lifestyle include movable pads that close off the nostrils when its head is underwater and a mouth that shuts completely (without the gap for the tongue seen on the mouths of land snakes).

Like the Siamese River Snake, Peringuey's Viper *(Bitis peringueyi)* lures its prey toward it. A desert snake, it buries itself in the sand with just its eyes and the tip of its tail visible. When it spots a lizard – its main prey – it wriggles the end of its tail. The lizard, mistaking the movement for that of an insect, rushes in to grab a meal but ends up becoming a meal itself.

Above right: Snakes swallow large prey very slowly, inching it down by moving the jaws on either side of their mouths independently.

Center right: Although the egg looks impossible to swallow, this Common Egg-eating Snake (Dasypeltis scabra) will have no problem eating its meal.

Below right: Fish feature in the diets of many snakes. Competition over meals like this is rare.

Opposite above: The Horned Viper (Cerastes cerates) buries itself in the sand of the deserts in which it lives to hide itself from prey. Not all individuals have horns. In those that do, they project as spines from the ridges above the eyes.

Opposite below: Peringuey's Viper (Bitis peringueyi) also lies beneath the sand to capture prey. This species has upward-pointing eyes which enable it to see prey even when the rest of its head is covered up.

Previous pages: The Gaboon Viper (Bitis gabonica, left) is superbly camouflaged. An ambush hunter, it lies in wait for prey among the fallen leaves on the rainforest floor. The Eyelash Viper (Bothriechis schlegeli, right), from Central America, hunts its prey in the trees.

Above: Pythons kill their prey by constriction before swallowing it. Contrary to popular belief, constricted prey is not crushed to death but suffocated, squeezed until it is no longer able to refill its lungs.

Top left: A Gaboon Viper (Bitis gabonica) in its natural habitat is very hard to spot. This large venomous snake inhabits tropical forests in Africa.

Top right: Without venom or powerful coils, many colubrid snakes eat small prey animals such as frogs, which can be killed by biting alone.

Opposite: The Royal Python (Python regius) lives wild in the savannah and wooded plains of Central and West Africa. A small python, averaging just 3ft 3in (1m) long, it hunts small mammals.

Other hunting techniques

Luring prey into range is a useful tactic that improves the chances of catching food. Most snakes that hunt by ambush, however, simply wait for prey to wander close enough to strike. The Gaboon Viper *(Bitis gabonica)* is one such snake. It lives in the rainforests of Central Africa and lies motionless on the ground amongst the leaf litter, sometimes for days on end. Its patterned scales provide it with such exquisite camouflage that it is practically impossible to see in the dappled light. Full grown adults are large enough to tackle young forest antelopes, although they usually settle for smaller prey. The Gaboon Viper disables and kills its victims with a massive dose of venom, which it injects through the longest fangs possessed by any snake. These huge, specialized teeth, like backward-curving hypodermic needles, can reach up to 2in (5cm) from base to tip.

Using venom is one of the most efficient methods snakes have evolved for dealing with prey. Even if their victims manage to struggle free, they rarely get far before the venom takes effect. Small animals are quickly killed and larger ones paralyzed or subdued enough to be swallowed without risk of injury to the snake.

Some other snakes kill their prey by suffocation. These snakes, known as constrictors, coil their bodies around the animals they catch, tightening their grip every time their victims breathe out. They do not crush their prey, as some people imagine, but make it impossible for their victims to refill their lungs. All of the world's largest snakes kill in this way. Some of them include other top predators on their list of prey. The Asiatic Rock Python *(Python molurus)*, for example, has been recorded killing and eating leopards, while the Yellow Anaconda *(Eunectes notaeus)* regularly feeds on the Yacare Caiman, a South American relative of the alligators and crocodiles.

Most snakes are neither venomous nor giants. The majority of these harmless species feed on rodents and other small mammals, their slender bodies giving them the great advantage over other predators of being able to enter the burrows of their prey. Other, tree-climbing species feed on lizards and take chicks from the nests of birds, again, including those out of reach of most other predators.

The smallest snakes of all, and the least known, feed on the larvae of termites and ants. Thread snakes, or worm snakes, as they are also called, spend most of their lives in the nests of their prey. Like other snakes, they feed infrequently on relatively large meals, gorging themselves with many larvae, then digesting their meals over a number of days. Slightly larger but with similar feeding habits are the blind snakes, which have also been little studied.

Forms of defense

While snakes have evolved to become feared predators in the animal kingdom, they have not had it all their own way. Many other animals feed on snakes, including wild pigs, mongooses, and several birds of prey.

In order to avoid being eaten, snakes have evolved a number of different means of defense. Some venomous snakes advertise the fact that they are dangerous with bright warning colors, while other, harmless snakes have evolved to mimic them. North America's kingsnakes and milk snakes, for example, have bright, alternating stripes of red, black and white or gold, making them hard to distinguish from the highly venomous coral snakes that share their home.

Rattlesnakes have got around the problem of advertising their venomousness without having to resort to bright colors, maintaining their excellent camouflage. Instead of visual cues, they use sound, generated by the rattle at the end of the tail, to warn predators to keep their distance. The

rattlesnake also uses its rattle to alert other large animals to its presence, in order to avoid being trodden on.

Another defense mechanism used by some snakes to avoid being eaten is to play dead. Many mammalian predators in particular leave dead animals alone, preferring instead to eat only animals that they have killed themselves. North America's Eastern Hognose Snake *(Heterodon platirhinos)* and the European Grass Snake *(Natrix natrix)* both employ this method, rolling on to their backs and lying still with their mouths open and tongues hanging out until the danger has passed.

Above: *If it feels threatened, the Grass Snake* (Natrix natrix) *feigns death. Surprisingly, this trick often works. Many predatory mammals are reluctant to eat prey that they have not killed themselves.*

Opposite: *Large and venomous, rattlesnakes are rightly feared. Nowadays, the widespread availability of antivenin means that they rarely kill people. Nevertheless, their bites can cause serious injury and permanent scars.*

Perhaps the most extreme example of evolution for defense affecting a snake's appearance and behavior is that of Africa's burrowing Two-headed Python *(Calabaria reinhardtii)*. This generally nocturnal forest dweller has a rounded end to its tail, which makes it look like the snake's head. The real head with its tiny eyes, on the other hand, is more pointed and looks like the tail. If threatened, the python coils itself up and sticks its tail out from the center of the coil, where any other snake would put its head. Should any predator attack, it invariably goes for the tail, thinking that it is the snake's head. This gives the real head end of the snake a chance to escape by trying to burrow out of danger. While it is doing this, the tail jumps about and lunges toward the attacker, mimicking the defensive lunges of a normal snake's head.

While these various forms of defense are far from foolproof, they often work against mammals and birds. However, one group of predators ignores them completely – other snakes. Several snake species specialize in preying on other snakes. The largest of these is the King Cobra *(Ophiophagus hannah)*, which is found in India and South-East Asia. Growing to over 16ft 5in (5m) long, it is more than a match for the smaller cobras and other venomous snakes that it hunts, and has no trouble swallowing them whole.

Another snake-eater, the Common Kingsnake *(Lampropeltis getula)* from North America, sometimes eats corn snakes that are longer than itself. Lacking venom, it kills its victims by constriction before swallowing them. The Common Kingsnake manages to force its prey into its body by squashing it up, so that the vertebral column of the snake it has eaten is bent into waves.

Right: *The Great Basin Rattlesnake* (Crotalus viridis lutosus) *inhabits the hot, dry south-western states of the USA. As with other rattlesnakes, the rattle at the end of the tail grows with age. This is a young individual.*

BREEDING AND YOUNG

The majority of snake species breed once a year. In temperate regions the process usually begins in spring, shortly after hibernation, but in the tropics breeding seasons vary considerably, with some species apparently not having any fixed breeding season at all.

When a female snake becomes ready to mate, she emits a scent from her skin and, in some species, from her anal glands. This attracts nearby males, which follow the scent trail toward her. The first to arrive is usually the one that gets to mate, although he may be displaced if a larger, stronger male appears soon after him. At the start of the breeding season the males of some species, such as the Western Diamondback Rattlesnake (Crotalus atrox), become aggressive toward one another and engage in combat, intertwining their bodies, with each trying to wrestle the other to the ground. The purpose of this is to establish dominance. Males that lose these battles experience a rise in stress hormones, which causes them to become jittery and lose interest in mating.

Before mating actually happens, there is a brief ritual courtship. In most species this involves the male rubbing the underside of his head along the female's flanks and back while moving slowly upward toward her head. This has the effect of calming the female and gets both sexes into a position where they are ready to mate.

Once mating has happened, the eggs begin to develop inside the female. In a few species females are able to store sperm and so fertilize several clutches from a single mating, but generally female snakes lay just one clutch in any given year. The time between mating and laying varies widely between species, from a few days to as much as two months. Eggs tend to be laid in a secluded crevice, animal's burrow or amongst rotting vegetation. After laying, most mothers desert their eggs but in some species they stay and guard them until they hatch. King Cobras (Ophiophagus hannah) actually build nest mounds for their eggs, scooping up piles of vegetation. The eggs are laid in a compartment at the bottom of the mound and the mother then excavates a second compartment above this, in which she waits as her young develop. The male also remains nearby and helps protect the nest mound from predators.

Pythons do not build nests but in many species the mother remains coiled around her eggs after laying. This behavior is also exhibited by several other kinds of snake. Female pythons have regular muscular contractions or tremors that help to keep the eggs warm but the main

reason that they coil around their eggs is to protect them. Containing everything that a young snake needs to develop, eggs are highly nutritious and actively sought out by many predators, particularly mammals.

One way to get around the problem of protecting eggs from predators is to avoid laying them altogether and instead give birth to live young. This behavior is particularly common among species from temperate regions, where it has the added advantage of ensuring that the young develop before birth under stable conditions. Eggs laid in these parts of the world may experience sudden fluctuations in temperature, but a female snake will do her best to avoid these by seeking shelter and so keep her temperature relatively high. Another group in which giving birth to live young is common is that of the sea snakes. For them the advantage is different – by giving birth to live young they avoid ever having to come out on to land.

Although bearing live young sounds very different from egg laying, in most snakes it is not. The vast majority of species that give birth to live young simply retain their eggs inside their bodies until they are ready to hatch. The processes of hatching and birth are almost simultaneous,

Top right: *Male rattlesnakes do battle, each trying to force the other to the ground. Males that lose these tussles tend to lose the drive to mate.*

Center right: *Gopher snakes* (Pituophis melanoleucus) *mate, their bodies intertwined. Sometimes, as here, the male holds the female's head during mating.*

Below right: *An adult Common Garter Snake. This species gives birth to between 4 and 80 live young.*

Opposite: *A female Children's Python* (Antaresia childreni) *from Australia lies coiled around her clutch of eggs.*

Previous pages: *A young pair of Common Garter Snakes (*Thamnophis sirtalis, *left) peer from spring woodland foliage. Before they gain their adult colors, Green Tree Pythons (*Morelia viridis) *might be better named Banana Tree Pythons, most being a beautiful yellow color.*

with the former happening just a very short time before the latter. A few species of snake, however, have a primitive form of placenta and nourish their young inside their bodies outside the egg, as mammals do. Among this small group are the garter snakes (*Thamnophis* species) from North America.

Starting out

Whether they are born or hatch from eggs, baby snakes look identical to their parents in everything apart from size. Hatchlings break out of their eggs, which have thin, leathery shells, with the aid of a tiny spike on the snout, known as the egg tooth. This drops off shortly after the young snake has emerged.

Newborn snakes are able to fend for themselves and soon leave the nest to go off in search of their first meal. All but the largest start out life by hunting invertebrates but quickly move on to larger prey. Young snakes grow rapidly and may double or even triple their size in a year. As with all reptiles, they continue to grow throughout life, although the rate of growth slows down considerably as they become older.

Life for young snakes is fraught with danger and few survive to adulthood. The main threat comes from the many predators that count them as food. For this reason most snakes lay big clutches of eggs or give birth to large numbers of young.

Top left: Common Garter Snakes in a breeding mass. This species hibernates communally and mates immediately after emerging in spring.

Center left: A Green Mamba (Dendroaspis angusticeps) emerges from its egg. Snakes lay eggs with leathery shells. Breaking out of them takes time but is made easier by the egg tooth, a tiny spike just visible in this picture.

Below left: A rattlesnake from South America, the Cascabel (Crotalus durissus), gives birth to live young.

Opposite: These newly-hatched Corn Snakes (Elaphe guttata) are almost perfect miniature replicas of their parents. Some snake species are identical to their parents in everything but size. Others differ from them in color.

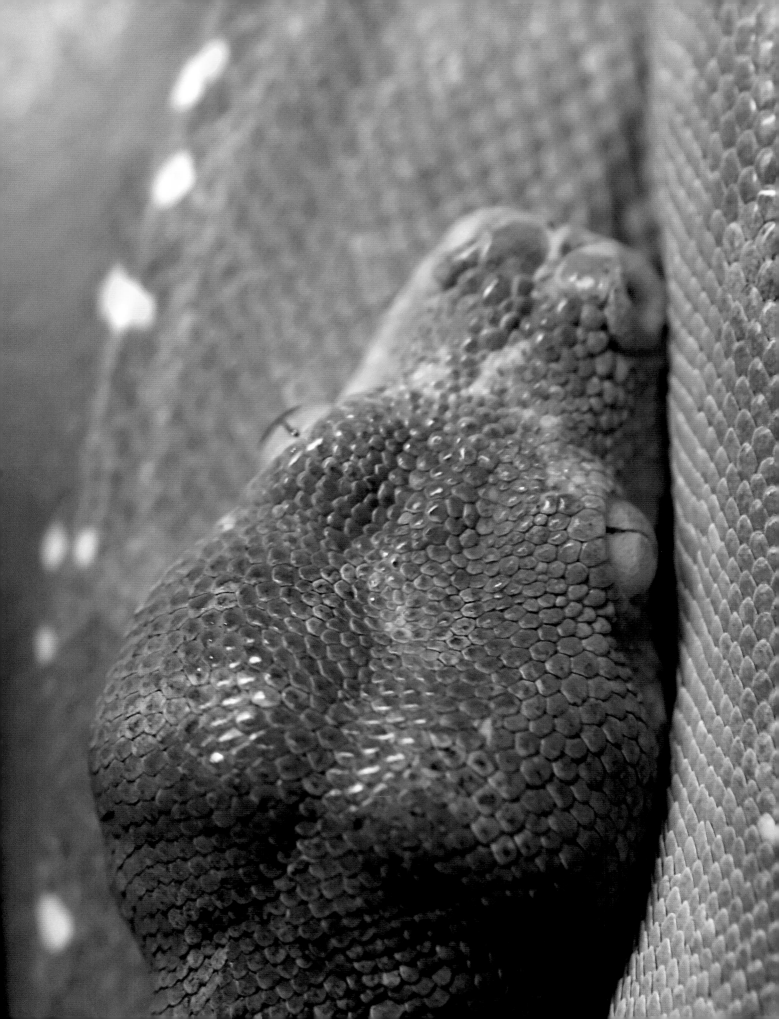

SNAKE FAMILIES

Snakes are classified by scientists into 19 different families. Three of those families are made up entirely of venomous snakes: the family Viperidae contains all of the world's vipers, Elapidae contains the cobras and their relatives, and Hydrophiidae contains the sea snakes. Boas and pythons have their own families.

Most other snakes belong to the family Colubridae. The scientific classification of snakes is based on anatomical characteristics and reflects their relatedness to one another. Many people, however, would group snakes by one factor – namely, how they kill their prey.

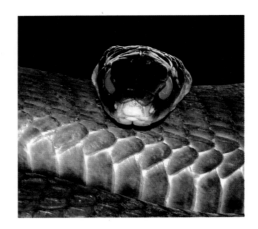

VENOMOUS SNAKES

Few animals strike more fear into the hearts of people than venomous snakes. Although only a relatively small number of species are deadly to humans, many can cause serious injury. At the very least, a bite from one of these snakes will cause significant pain.

Snakes did not evolve venom to defend themselves, however. Its true function is to kill or disable their prey. Venom reduces the risk of injury to a snake from its prey struggling and it also makes it much less likely to get away.

Snake venom works in one of two ways. Neurotoxic venom acts on the victim's nervous system and causes death either through heart failure or breathing problems due to paralysis. Hemotoxic venom attacks the circulatory system and muscle tissue. It usually causes death by a collapse in the victim's blood pressure. People or animals that survive a hemotoxic bite are usually left with serious scarring.

The venom produced by each species of snake is unique, containing varying amounts of a large number of different toxic enzymes. Broadly speaking, however, sea snakes and elapids, such as cobras, have neurotoxic venom. Hemotoxic venom is produced by vipers and their relatives.

The venom of some species is more dangerous to humans than that of others. The most potent venom of all is that of the Fierce Snake or Inland Taipan (*Oxyuranus microlepidotus*), which comes from the deserts and other arid regions of central Australia. Its venom is around 50 times more potent than that of the Indian Cobra (*Naja naja*), a distant relative which is itself a potentially deadly snake.

By coincidence, all ten of the world's most venomous snakes live in Australia. Deaths from snakebites in that country, however, are rare. This is partly because of the rarity of encounters with these snakes in the wild, and partly because of the wide availability of antivenin. Made using the venom of captive snakes, which are 'milked' to extract it, antivenin has been developed to combat the bites of all Australian snakes, as well as many other venomous snakes around the world.

Most people killed by snakebites die in countries where antivenin is scarce. Snakes kill upward of 10,000 people every year in India and according to the World Health Organization account for around 40,000 deaths annually worldwide. The most dangerous snake in terms of the number of people it kills is the Saw-scaled or Carpet Viper (*Echis carinatus*). It is found from West Africa through the Middle East to India and Sri Lanka and is reported to account for 8000 fatalities every year in Asia alone. A small snake, it

Above: A rattlesnake is milked for its venom. Venom collected in this way is used to make antivenin, which is used to treat snake bites.

Top: The Gaboon Viper (Bitis gabonica) *has a huge mouth and the longest fangs of any snake. In this picture, taken mid-strike, the fangs are being pulled forward into position.*

Opposite: A Cape Cobra (Naja nivea) *from southern Africa raises its hood menacingly. The hood is opened by muscles attached to extended ribs.*

Previous pages: The Black Mamba (Dendroaspis polylepis, *left) is Africa's largest venomous snake. The Horned Viper* (Cerastes cerastes, *right) from north Africa, Israel and Arabia is also highly dangerous.*

nevertheless has the most potent venom of any viper and is aggressive and quick to strike if disturbed.

Venomous giants

A distant relative of the Saw-scaled Viper, the Gaboon Viper *(Bitis gabonica)* holds another record. It injects more venom per bite on average than any other snake – a massive half a pint (around 475mg). Less than a quarter of that amount would be needed to kill a full-grown man outright, but attacks by this species are rare. This is not because it is unaggressive but because it rarely encounters people, living deep in the rainforest of West Africa.

The Gaboon Viper is the world's second heaviest venomous snake. The heaviest is North America's Eastern Diamondback Rattlesnake *(Crotalus adamanteus)*. Although less bulky, it grows much longer, reaching more than 6ft 7in (2m) from nose to tail, and weighing as much as 34lb (15kg). Despite the availability of antivenin for its bites, the Eastern Diamondback Rattlesnake kills several people in North America every year. Although it possesses a rattle to warn larger animals to stay away, it does not always use this and sometimes strikes before it has even been noticed.

Closely related to the rattlesnakes, the bushmasters of Central and South America are perhaps even more feared. Like their North American cousins, these pit vipers are deadly and even more likely to strike without warning. The Common Bushmaster *(Lachesis muta)* is the longest venomous snake in the Western Hemisphere, growing to more than 11ft 6in (3.5m) long. Two other species exist, the Central American Bushmaster *(Lachesis stenophrys)* and the Black-headed Bushmaster *(Lachesis melanocephala)*. The latter was only identified as a separate species in 1986.

Not all venomous snakes are giants. In fact many are quite small. The common European Adder *(Vipera berus)*, for example, rarely exceeds 2ft (60cm) long. The smallest of all venomous snakes is the Spotted Dwarf Adder *(Bitis schneideri)* from Namibia. It averages just 8in (21cm) in length and feeds mainly on frogs and small geckoes.

The principal function of venom is to aid in hunting, but for those snakes that have evolved it, venom serves a very important secondary role in defense. The phrase 'once bitten, twice shy' could hardly be more appropriately applied than to these creatures and some venomous snakes go out of their way to avoid having to bite in the first place, advertising the fact that they are dangerous with bright warning colors.

For one group of venomous snakes, the defensive role has caused the evolution of a unique form of behavior. Spitting cobras fire their venom into the faces of larger animals that attack them, causing their tormentors to go temporarily blind. The venom is sprayed from the forward-facing holes at the tips of the fangs and is helped on its way by a gust of air as the snake exhales. There are 11 different species of spitting cobras altogether. Four of these live in Africa and the other seven in Asia. When hunting, all use their fangs to inject venom into their prey in the usual way.

Cobras and vipers are front-fanged snakes. Both have two long fangs at the front of their mouths which they use to inject venom. Although the structure of these fangs differs slightly between the two groups, they work in the same way, channeling venom down from large glands in the roof of the mouth. Normally these fangs are folded back flat against the palate, but at the moment the snake opens its mouth to strike, they are pulled forward and into position.

Back-fanged snakes, as their name suggests, have their fangs at the back of their mouths. This makes them less dangerous to humans as they are rarely able to break the skin and inject their venom, unless they bite on a finger or toe. Back-fanged venomous snakes include the Boomslang (*Dispholidus typus*) and Twig Snake (*Thelotornis capensis*), which both come from Africa, and the mangrove snakes (*Boiga* species), which range from Africa through Asia, and Australia to Polynesia.

The world's venomous snakes are not just restricted to land. All the 50 or so species of sea snake produce venom, which they use to kill the fish on which they feed. Sea snakes inject their venom using fangs at the front of the mouth. These are shorter than in land-living front-fanged snakes but are long enough to puncture human skin. Although encounters with most sea snakes are rare, one species, the Beaked Sea Snake (*Enhydrina schistosa*), regularly enters estuaries and tidal creeks. In South-East Asia its bites cause several human deaths every year.

Above: *The Boomslang* (Dispholidus typus) *grows to around 4ft (1.25m) long. Slender and agile, it spends most of its time in the trees, where it hunts birds, chameleons and other relatively small prey.*

Opposite above: *If threatened, a Spitting Cobra* (Naja *and* Hemachatus *species) will shoot its venom into the face of its tormentor. These snakes also inject venom in the more traditional way to subdue their prey.*

Opposite below: *The Adder* (Vipera berus) *is Britain's only venomous snake. The other two species native to Britain are the Grass Snake* (Natrix natrix) *and the Smooth Snake* (Coronella austriaca). *All three also live in continental Europe but are absent from Ireland.*

Above: *The Gold-ringed Cat Snake* (Boiga dendrophila) *is a type of mangrove snake. It inhabits coastal mangrove forests and the riverine forests that adjoin them, hunting in the branches at night for birds, lizards and other small prey.*

Top: *All of the world's sea snakes are venomous. They are most common in coastal waters, where they hunt fish, often catching and killing their prey as it hides in rock crevices or gaps in coral reefs.*

Following pages: *Also known as the Asian Sand Viper, the Leaf-nosed Viper* (Eristicophis macmahonii) *is a desert species found in Iran, Afghanistan and Pakistan. Although small, averaging around 2ft (60cm) long, it is potentially deadly to humans.*

Above: The Copperhead or Highland Moccasin (Agkistrodon contortrix) *is the most common venomous snake in the eastern USA. Its bite, although not fatal, can be extremely painful and cause permanent scarring and tissue damage. As with most venomous snakes, it does not bite humans unless provoked. Most bites are caused when people try to kill it or pick it up.*

Right: As its name suggests, the Prairie Rattlesnake (Crotalus viridis) *is an inhabitant of the Great Plains and the lands they used to cover, occurring over a broad band of territory from southern Canada to northern Mexico. Potentially deadly, it is the most widespread rattlesnake in the USA and the only one likely to be encountered in many states.*

Following pages: Although not found in the USA, the Eyelash Viper (Bothriechis schlegeli) *does occur in southern Mexico. This tropical species is also known as the Eyelash Palm Pit Viper.*

CONSTRICTORS

Constrictors are snakes that kill their prey by squeezing, wrapping their coils around it, and tightening their grip until it is unable to breathe. All the world's biggest snakes are constrictors from tropical and subtropical parts of the globe.

The largest snake of all is South America's Green Anaconda *(Eunectes murinus)*. This monstrous predator can weigh more than three full grown men and reach at least 29ft 6in (9m) long. Tales have been told of even bigger specimens lurking deep in the jungle. The longest ever claimed to have been measured was found by a petroleum expedition in Colombia in 1944. It was said to have been 37ft 5in (11.4m) from nose to tail, although there was no photographic or other evidence to back up the claim. More reliable, but still never independently verified, is the report made by the late scientist Vincent Roth. He claimed to have shot and killed an anaconda measuring 33ft 10in (10.3m) in Guyana (then British Guyana).

What is beyond doubt is that the Green Anaconda is the world's largest snake. Some pythons have been reliably measured that are longer but none come close to this boa for sheer bulk. The reason it is able to grow so large is its primarily aquatic lifestyle. Hunting caimans, capybaras and other large animals in swamps and the backwaters of large rivers, the adults rarely leave the water except to travel to new hunting grounds or to breed.

The Green Anaconda is by far the biggest and best known member of its genus but three other species of anaconda exist. The Yellow Anaconda *(Eunectes notaeus)* reaches an average length of around 9ft 10in (3m). It lives farther south than the Green Anaconda, ranging as far as Uruguay and northern Argentina. The Dark-Spotted or De Schauensee's Anaconda *(Eunectes deschauenseei)* is restricted to north-eastern Brazil, around Ilha Marajo in the mouth of the Amazon, while the Bolivian Anaconda *(Eunectes beniensis)* was only identified in 2002 and is still being studied. All three have similar lifestyles to their larger cousin.

Anacondas are not the only large snakes in South America. The Boa Constrictor *(Boa constrictor)* grows up to 14ft 9in (4.5m) long. This widespread predator occurs from Mexico to Argentina and has been split by scientists into seven different subspecies, which vary in size and color. Boa Constrictors feed on smaller prey than anacondas and live in a far wider range of habitats. In Peru, they are found on arid, rocky plains and they are also common in savannah and other types of grassland. In forests, Boa Constrictors do much of their hunting in trees.

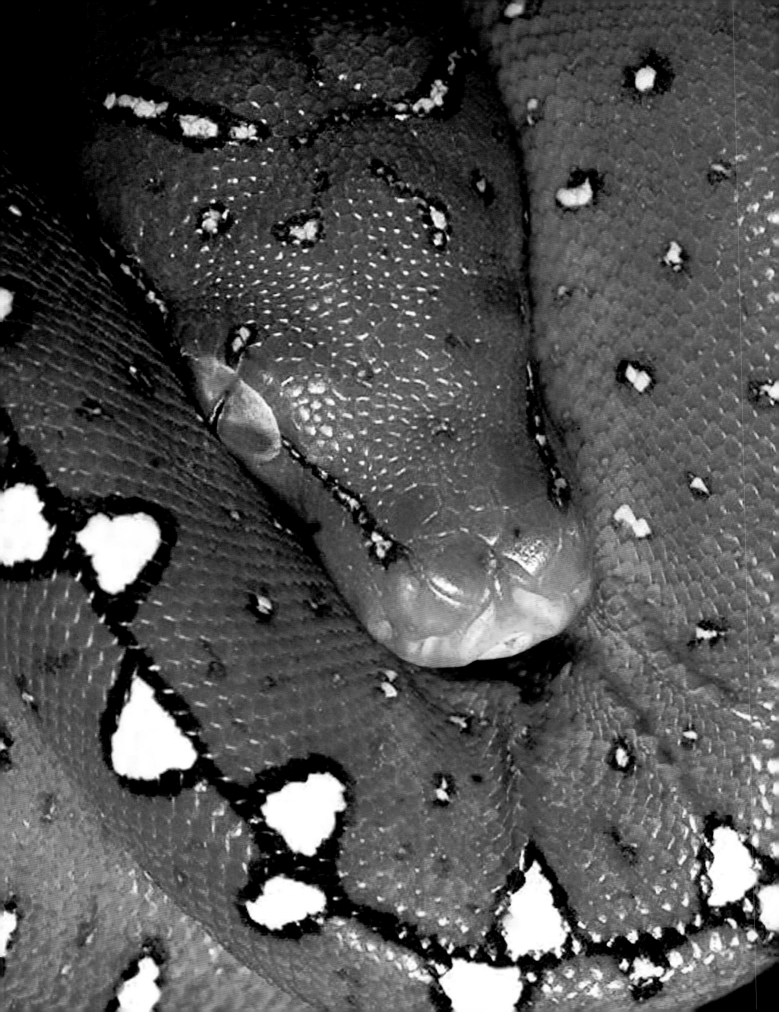

Above: The Boa Constrictor (Boa constrictor) *is one of South and Central America's most common large snakes, occurring in various habitats.*

Top: The Yellow Anaconda (Eunectes notaeus) *often basks on land but rarely strays far from the water in which it hunts.*

Opposite: Most young Green Tree Pythons are a vivid yellow but in some regions they are red. The colors correspond to those of locally abundant arboreal flowers, around which the young snakes lie in wait for prey.

Previous pages: The Reticulated Python (Python reticulatus, *left) has beautifully patterned skin. Like that of the Green tree Python* (Morelia viridis, *opposite) it helps to camouflage the snake from potential prey.*

A match for the Boa Constrictor in size, the Cuban Boa *(Epicrates angulifer)* inhabits broken woodland and grassy plains. In recent decades it has become scarce as its natural habitat has been turned over to farmland. This has increased its encounters with local people, who tend to react to snakes by grabbing a machete and killing them. The Cuban Boa is considered threatened with extinction in the wild but has been found to breed well in captivity, so its future as a species looks safe.

Common beauty

One boa that is far from endangered is the Emerald Tree Boa *(Corallus caninus)*. This beautiful snake is found throughout the Amazon Basin, from Bolivia and Peru through Brazil, and Colombia to Venezuela. A nocturnal predator, it spends the day coiled up with its body draped over a branch but becomes active as the sun dips below the horizon, setting out in search of small mammals and roosting birds. Like all boas, it has heat receptors around its snout which enable it to 'see' its prey in total darkness. It has even been known to catch bats on the wing, striking down at them while holding onto a branch with its prehensile tail.

Most boas are restricted to Central and South America but a few live thousands of miles away. The Madagascan Ground Boa *(Acrantophis madagascariensis)* is one such species. Growing up to 13ft 2in (4m) long, it is Madagascar's largest snake. The Madagascan Ground Boa closely resembles the Boa Constrictor in both appearance and behavior. Like that species, it is nocturnal, becoming active at dusk. It spends the daylight hours lying still, usually beneath the shelter of a fallen log or in bushy scrub. Sadly, along with many other Madagascan animals, it has become endangered as the dry, deciduous forests it inhabits have disappeared, lost to slash and burn agriculture.

Record breakers

Boas are often considered the New World equivalent of pythons, although the Madagascan Ground Boa is obviously an exception to this rule. Pythons are found throughout much of Africa, Asia, and Australia. There are 36 species altogether, ranging in size from the 2ft 4in (70cm) long

Anthill or Pygmy Python *(Antaresia perthensis)* of Australia to the Reticulated Python *(Python reticulatus)*, the longest snake in the world.

The Reticulated Python lives in South-East Asia and on several islands in the far West Pacific. It is found in a wide range of habitats, from open grassland to rainforest. The Reticulated Python is a formidable snake that can grow to a great length. The longest ever reliably recorded measured 32ft 2in (10m) from nose to tail. It was shot and measured in northern Sulawesi, Indonesia, in 1912. There have been several records of this python killing and eating people, although instances of this are extremely rare.

A close runner-up for the title of world's longest snake, the African Rock Python *(Python sebae)* can grow up to 32ft 2in (9.8m) long. This species is most common in wooded savannah and tends to be found near water. The African Rock Python often spends much of the daytime basking and normally only hunts at night. Its prey ranges from rats and other small mammals to antelopes. As with other pythons, it has heat sensitive pits along its upper lip, which it uses to locate and target its victims.

With its beautiful markings the Royal Python *(Python regius)* is one of the most commonly seen snakes in captivity. In the wild it is found in West and Central Africa, being most common in savannah habitats and lightly wooded plains. The Royal Python is a relatively small constrictor, averaging around just 3ft 3in (1m) in length. A nocturnal predator, it hunts small mammals and usually spends the day hiding out in their burrows. If caught in the open, it will coil itself tightly up into a ball, with its head tucked into the middle. This habit, which works as quite an effective defense mechanism against most larger predators, has earned it the alternative common name of Ball Python.

Another common West African python, but one that looks very different, is the Two-headed Python *(Calabaria reinhardtii)*. This snake, which inhabits rainforests, is also

Left: Color mutations occur in nature but snakes that possess them rarely reach adulthood, as they stand out, making them easy for predators to spot. This Royal or Ball Python (Python regius) *was bred in captivity.*

known as the Burrowing Python for its habit of tunneling through the loose soil and leaf litter of the forest floor, searching for the rodents and other small vertebrates on which it feeds. Like the Royal Python, it grows to about 3ft 3in (1m) long.

While most pythons are active predators that go out in search of prey at night, the Blood Python *(Python curtus)* is an ambush predator that waits for food to find it. In its lifestyle this python from Malaysia and Indonesia mirrors the anacondas. It too spends most of its time in the waters of swamps and rainforest streams, lying in wait for unsuspecting mammals and birds. Although it rarely grows to much more than 6ft 7in (2m) long, the Blood Python has an unusually thick body, even thicker, relative to its length, than those of its South American counterparts.

Pythons down under

Pythons are common in Australia, with no fewer than 15 species living there. The most familiar of these snakes is the Carpet Python *(Morelia spilota)*. It is named for the beautiful and intricate patterns on its skin, which vary between the six different subspecies. The Carpet Python is an adaptable hunter, finding prey both on the ground and in the trees. In New Guinea it competes for food with the Green Tree Python *(Chondropython viridis)*. This snake is remarkably similar in appearance and habits to the Emerald Tree Boa, which lives on the other side of the world.

Like the Emerald Tree Boa, the Green Tree Python hunts in the branches of rainforest trees by night and spends the day coiled in the same pose as its South American counterpart. It also makes use of a prehensile tail. The adults of both species are very similar in color and so, even more remarkably, are their young, starting out life yellow or red, and gradually turning green as they grow older. The only significant difference between the species is their breeding systems: the Green Tree Python lays eggs while the Emerald Tree Boa gives birth to live young.

Right: The Woma Python (Aspidites ramsayi) *is an endangered Australian species. It lacks the heat sensitive pits possessed by most other pythons.*

Above: *There are six different subspecies of Boa Constrictor, each geographically isolated from the others. This young individual is a Trinidad Red-tail Boa Constrictor (Boa constrictor constrictor) from the Caribbean island after which it is named.*

Following pages: The Carpet Python (Morelia spilotes) *inhabits much of northern and eastern Australia, and the island of New Guinea. It tends to be most active at night, hunting prey on the ground and in the trees by detecting its body heat.*

OTHER SNAKES

Most snakes are neither venomous nor constricting. Instead, they hunt small creatures that are easily overpowered by biting alone. Occasionally these snakes have saliva that is toxic to their prey, but all are completely harmless to humans.

The vast majority of these other snakes – indeed the majority of all snakes – belong to the family Colubridae. Colubrids are by far the most common snakes on all the continents apart from Australia, where the cobra family (Elapidae) predominates. Although the Colubridae has a few venomous back-fanged members, such as the Boomslang (*Dispholidus typus*), Montpellier Snake (*Malpolon monspessulanus*) and flying snakes (*Chrysopelea* species), these make up a tiny minority of the 1700 or so species in the family.

One of the most common and widespread colubrids is the Grass Snake (*Natrix natrix*), which occurs in parts of North America, through most of Europe and eastward into central Asia. It has the distinction of being the largest reptile native to Britain, growing up to 5ft 9in (1.75m) long. The Grass Snake lives mainly on a diet of frogs and is an excellent swimmer. Another favorite prey, the Common Toad (*Bufo bufo*) has evolved an interesting behavioral response to this

snake, standing high on its toes and puffing out its body to make it appear bigger than it actually is. While this defensive bluff is not foolproof, it does often work.

A close relative of the Grass Snake, the Checkered Keelback (*Natrix piscator*), has a similar lifestyle but a different range. It too feeds mainly on frogs, although it also catches fish. The Checkered Keelback ranges from western Pakistan to Vietnam, and spends much of its time in the water. In common with many other largely aquatic snakes, it has its nostrils placed high on its snout, enabling it to take a breath without having to lift its whole head above the surface. This both helps it avoid the attention of predators such as herons and improves its chances of catching a meal. With its eyes always under the water, it never misses an opportunity to strike at passing fish.

Most snakes of the genus *Natrix* hunt fish or amphibians. Among them are the Dice Snake (*Natrix tessellata*) from southern Europe, and the Viperine Water Snake (*Natrix maura*) from the western Mediterranean regions of Europe and North Africa. Other colubrids, however, tend to find their prey on land.

In North America the most common members of this family are the garter snakes. The Common Garter Snake

Previous pages: The Grass Snake (Natrix natrix, left) often hunts in water. Frogs and other amphibians make up a large part of its diet. The Black-necked Garter Snake (Thamnophis cyrtopsis, right) occurs from Utah and Colorado, USA, to Guatemala. A small snake, it also specializes in catching amphibians.

Left: Although predators themselves, most snakes have predators of their own. Herons and other large birds such as storks and some eagles frequently catch and eat snakes.

Below: Asia's Beauty Snake (Elaphe taeniura) is well named, its scales ranging through virtually every color of the rainbow. A relatively large species, growing up to 7ft (2.15m) long, it feeds mainly on rodents.

*Above: North America's Gopher Snake (*Pituophis catenifer*) hunts small mammals, catching them both on the surface and in their burrows.*

*Top: The Common Corn Snake (*Elaphe guttata guttata*) occurs throughout the southeastern USA and, like the Gopher Snake, feeds mainly on rodents. It is one of two subspecies of* Elaphe guttata*. The other, the Great Plains Rat Snake (*Elaphe gutatta emoryi*), ranges from Nebraska through Texas to northern Mexico.*

(Thamnophis sirtalis), as its name suggests, is the most abundant of all. A small snake, rarely exceeding 2ft 2in (66cm) long, the Common Garter Snake is among the hardiest of all reptiles and has the most northerly range of any snake in the Western Hemisphere. Wherever it is found, it is invariably the last snake to go into hibernation and the first to emerge in the spring. Sometimes it is even seen out in the open while there is still snow on the ground.

The Common Garter Snake feeds on slugs, earthworms, small lizards and salamanders. It mates during April and May and gives birth to a brood of live young three months later. Most females bear around 25 young but older, larger individuals may have as many as 78.

The Common Garter Snake is unusual among reptiles in that it actually seems to dislike hot weather. In the height of summer it is rarely seen, preferring to shelter in shady areas, usually near water.

False colors

The Red Milk Snake *(Lampropeltis triangulum syspila)*, by contrast, is often seen basking. This harmless colubrid mimics the highly venomous coral snakes that share its range in the eastern USA and the south-east of Canada. As a result, it is usually left alone by predators.

The Red Milk Snake feeds mainly on small mammals, as do many North American members of this family. This makes them popular with farmers. The Gopher Snake *(Pituophis catenifer)* specializes in hunting burrowing rodents. Averaging about 3ft 11in (1.2m) long, it is found throughout much of the western USA and Canada, occurring in most habitats apart from high mountains. There are several different subspecies, some of which go by different common names. Like many other burrowing snakes, the Gopher Snake has an enlarged rostral shield (the scale at the tip of its snout) which, together with the other scales of the wedge-shaped head, slopes upward and over the eyes. This gives the whole head a smooth surface free of bumps and sharp angles, which aids the snake's movement underground.

Although many snakes hiss, the Gopher Snake is notable for the volume it achieves. A special membrane in front of the windpipe amplifies the sound that the snake makes by vibrating rhythmically when it exhales. The hisses the Gopher Snake makes when it is agitated can be heard from several hundred yards away.

Named for its dark colored, slender body, the Coachwhip Snake *(Masticophis flagellum)* is one of North America's longest snakes, sometimes exceeding 8ft 2in (2.5m). It feeds mainly on lizards, small mammals, and birds but occasionally kills and eats other snakes, including young rattlesnakes. The Coachwhip Snake is found in Mexico and the southern states of the USA. If it feels threatened, it is quick to flee and is a very fast mover, disappearing into scrub in the blink of an eye. This habit is shared with the smaller and aptly named racers *(Coluber* species) which live alongside it and in many other parts of the world.

Up in the branches

Not all colubrids are aquatic or restricted to hunting on the ground. Some species also find food in the trees. The Four-lined Snake *(Elaphe quatuorlineata)*, for example, is an excellent climber and includes nestlings and baby squirrels among its prey. This snake grows up to 6ft (1.8m) long, making it one of Europe's largest. It lives in Italy, the Balkan Peninsula and Turkey, as well as parts of the Middle East.

Perhaps the most arboreal of all the non-venomous colubrids are the egg-eating snakes. These specialists are mainly confined to Africa, with just one species living outside that continent, in India. Egg-eating snakes spend most of their time roving through the branches in search of birds' nests. Although vision plays an important part in their finding food, they also seem to be able to locate eggs by smell, using their flickering tongues to lead them to hidden clutches. Egg-eating snakes themselves reproduce by laying eggs but are unusual in that they lay them separately rather than altogether in one spot.

Although the family Colubridae is vast, it does not contain all of the world's smaller non-venomous snakes. More than 200 species fall outside it. These are the bizarre thread snakes and their cousins the blind snakes. Thread snakes include some of the world's smallest vertebrates. Some are so tiny that they can curl up on a small coin.

Left: *The San Francisco Garter Snake* (Thamnophis sirtalis tetrataenia) *is an endangered subspecies of the Common Garter Snake and is found only in California's San Mateo County.*

Opposite: *The Eastern Racer* (Coluber constrictor) *occurs throughout the USA east of the Rockies, as well as parts of Canada and most of Mexico, Guatemala and Belize. Like the Boa Constrictor* (Boa constrictor) *farther south, it varies greatly in color across its range and has been split into several different subspecies.*

Left: This Black Rat Snake (Elaphe obsoleta) *is a complete albino. Albinos lack the dark pigment melanin and can be told apart from animals with other forms of reduced pigmentation by the fact that they have pink eyes. Because they stand out, albino snakes are at a serious disadvantage in the wild. However, they are greatly sought after by specialist pet traders and collectors.*

Following pages: The Black-skinned Parrot Snake (Leptophis ahaetulla) *is an arboreal species from the tropics of South America. A slender stealth hunter, it preys mainly on tree frogs, which it catches by day.*

SNAKE FACTS

The first snakes appeared when there were dinosaurs still roaming the Earth. Although they have diversified a great deal since then, they have retained their basic body shape, a testament to its adaptability in the face of evolutionary pressure. Today there are snakes on every continent apart from Antarctica, living in habitats that range from termite mounds to the tops of rainforest trees. Altogether, there are around 2500 snake species. This represents almost half of the world's living reptiles and is more than all the world's mammals, barring rodents, put together.

SNAKE SNIPPETS

• The world's largest snake is the Green Anaconda (*Eunectes murinus*) of South America. It can reach lengths of more than 29ft 6in (9m) and weigh almost a quarter of a ton. The Reticulated Python (*Python reticulatus*) from South-East Asia grows slightly longer, up to 32ft 10in (10m), but is not so bulky and weighs considerably less.

• The world's smallest snake is the Lesser Antillean Threadsnake (*Leptotyphlops bilineata*). It rarely exceeds 4in (10cm) long and has a body so slender that it could fit through the hole in a standard pencil with the lead taken out.

• A snake's skeleton contains a string of vertebrae (bones that make up the spine). Typically, there are more than 120 in the body and tail and in some species as many as 585.

• All ten of the world's most venomous snakes live in Australia. The most dangerous of all is the Fierce Snake or Inland Taipan (*Oxyuranus microlepidotus*). Its venom is around 50 times as potent as that of the Indian Cobra (*Naja naja*), itself a potentially deadly snake.

• In most venomous snakes, the fangs work like hypodermic needles. When a victim is bitten, venom is forced down through these hollow teeth. In vipers, the fangs are folded against the roof of the mouth when not in use. Cobras and their relatives have fixed fangs.

• Australia is the only continent to have more venomous snake species than non-venomous ones. People in India, however, are far more likely to be killed by snakes than people in Australia. India has the greatest number of deaths from snakebites of any country in the world, with more than 10,000 people being killed there by venomous snakes each year.

• The people of certain islands in the Ryukyu Chain, south of Japan, suffer more snakebites than anyone else in the world. On average, one in 500 people is bitten by a snake there every year. Everyone who lives in the area has at least a one in seven chance of being bitten by a snake in their lifetime.

• The Black Mamba (*Dendroaspis polylepis*) of Africa is the world's fastest snake. This deadly venomous species has been recorded traveling at up to 12mph (19km/h) in short bursts, three times the speed of a person walking.

• The Gaboon Viper *(Bitis gabonica)* from Equatorial Africa produces more venom than any other snake in the world. The world's second heaviest venomous snake, it injects an average of half a pint (around 475mg) with every bite. The Gaboon Viper also has the longest fangs of any snake, reaching 2in (5cm) from base to tip.

• Pythons, boas and pit vipers (including rattlesnakes) all possess pit organs, which can detect the heat given off by other animals. Pit organs enable these snakes to effectively 'see' the thermal outline of their prey, allowing them to hunt at night when they themselves are hidden by darkness.

• A rattlesnake's rattle is made up of a series of loosely linked interlocking chambers. When shaken, these vibrate against one another to create the snake's distinctive warning sound. Only the bottom button of the rattle is firmly attached to the tail.

• Snakes have been both demonized and worshipped. In Christianity, the snake played the part of the Devil in the Garden of Eden, proffering the temptation that led to the fall from grace. In Hinduism, however, snakes are venerated and in some traditional African religions snakes were actually treated as gods. Quetzalcoatl, the supreme god of Central America's Toltec and Aztec civilizations, was believed to be a feathered serpent.

• Snakes have relatively short lives compared with some other reptiles. The oldest snake on record, a captive Boa Constrictor *(Boa constrictor)* called Popeye, died at the age of 40 years, 3 months and 14 days in Philadelphia Zoo. By contrast Tu'i Malila, a Madagascan Radiated Tortoise *(Geochelone radiata)* presented to the King of Tonga by Captain James Cook, lived until she was 188 years old, finally passing away in 1965.

• Snakes are incredible survivors and can go for great lengths of time without food. In nature, most feed at least every few weeks but if necessary some can fast for months at a time. The longest fast ever recorded for a snake was three years and three months, achieved by an Okinawa Habu *(Trimeresurus flavoviridis)*, a type of Asian pit viper. This fast was enforced as part of a scientific experiment, carried out in Japan. After the experiment was ended, the snake was found to have lost over 60 percent of its body weight, but, amazingly, it had actually increased in length. Once measured, it was fed and gradually made a complete recovery to full health.

• Sea snakes can stay underwater on a single breath for more than three hours if necessary. One in five of all dives by sea snakes lasts more than an hour.

Above: Rattlesnakes will sound a distinctive warning when disturbed.
Top: The Royal Python curls into a ball as defense against large predators.
Opposite: The USA's Common Corn Snake is docile and non-venomous.

SNAKE DIRECTORY

Superfamily Henophidia
Family Aniliidae
Common name Pipe snakes
Distinguishing features The single member of this family, the Red Pipe Snake or Burrowing False Coral Snake (*Anilius scytale*), has a robust and solid skull and a head the same width as the rest of its body. Its eyes are greatly reduced and lie beneath large scales, which protect them as it burrows through the soil in search of its prey. This species is ovoviviparous, meaning that it bears live young which hatch from eggs inside its body just before the moment of birth. The skeleton has a vestigial pelvic girdle and spurs protrude through the scales in the position where a lizard's hind legs would normally be.
Number of species 1
Largest species The Red Pipe Snake is the only Aniliid snake and reaches a maximum length of 2ft 4in (70cm).
Smallest species Being the only Aniliid snake, the Red Pipe Snake is also the smallest member of its family.
Distribution The Red Pipe Snake is a relatively widespread species, occurring throughout most of tropical South America east of the Andes. It is also found on the islands of Trinidad and Tobago.
Principal habitats A burrowing snake, the Red Pipe Snake lives in the loose soil and leaf litter of tropical rainforest.
Principal prey This snake feeds mainly on reptiles and amphibians, particularly other burrowing snakes, amphisbaenids (legless burrowing lizards) and caecilians (legless burrowing amphibians). It also eats burrowing insects and their larvae.
Most endangered species The Red Pipe Snake is not considered to be threatened.

Superfamily Henophidia
Family Anomochilus
Common name Dwarf pipe snakes
Distinguishing features The dwarf pipe snakes, also known as false blind snakes, are considered by most biologists to be the most primitive living snakes of all. They have blunt heads the same width as their cylindrical bodies – a common adaptation to a burrowing lifestyle – and short tails (the tail of a snake being the part that extends beyond the anus). Their mouths and eyes are unusually small.
Number of species 2
Largest species Both of the dwarf pipe snakes, Leonard's Pipe Snake (*Anomochilus leonardi*) and Weber's Pipe Snake (*Anomochilus weberi*) attain a similar maximum length of around 1ft 2in (36cm).
Smallest species There are currently so few records of these snakes that it cannot be accurately determined which of the two is smaller on average.
Distribution Weber's Pipe Snake is found on the islands of Sumatra and Borneo. Leonard's Pipe Snake is known mainly from a few sites in Peninsular Malaysia, although some specimens have also been recovered from the far north-east of Borneo.
Principal habitats The lives of these snakes are very poorly understood but they are thought to be burrowers that find their prey in leaf litter and soil. Both species have been found only in tropical rainforest.
Principal prey The feeding habits of these snakes are unknown but they are assumed to eat invertebrates such as worms and insect larvae, found in the soil.
Most endangered species Leonard's Pipe Snake is not considered threatened but it is the less common and widespread of the two dwarf pipe snakes.

Superfamily Henophidia
Family Boidae
Common name Boas
Distinguishing features Boas are considered among the more primitive snake families. They have two lungs (the majority of snakes have just one) and their skeletons show the remnants of pelvic bones and hind legs. They include many large snakes and all kill their prey by constriction. Boas lack teeth on their premaxilla (the bone that makes up the very front part of the skull and upper jaw), whereas pythons have teeth on that bone. This is the main anatomical feature biologists use to separate the two families. The other main difference between these two groups is that boas give birth to live young, whereas pythons lay eggs.
Number of species 47
Largest species The Green Anaconda (*Eunectes murinus*) is not only the largest boa but the largest of all snakes, growing up to at least 29ft 6in (9m) long and weighing as much as 500lb (225kg). The Reticulated Python (*Python reticulatus*), although longer, is much more slender.
Smallest species The Arabian Sand Boa (*Eryx jayakari*) and Elegant Sand Boa (*Eryx elegans*) officially tie for the title of smallest boa. Both have a maximum length of just 1ft 4in (40cm).
Distribution The majority of boa species live in South America, Central America and the Caribbean. Three species live in North America. Other boas occur in Fiji, New Guinea, the Solomon Islands, Madagascar, Central Asia, India, North-East Africa, and Arabia.
Principal habitats Boas live in a wide range of habitats, from tropical rainforest to deserts.
Principal prey All boas feed largely or exclusively on vertebrate animals. Prey ranges from birds, lizards, and other snakes to large mammals.
Most endangered species The three Madagascan boas, the Madagascan Ground Boa (*Acrantophis madagascariensis*), Madagascan Tree Boa (*Sanzinia madagascariensis*) and Dumeril's Boa (*Acrantophis dumerili*), are all listed as Vulnerable by the IUCN (International Union for the Conservation of Nature and Natural Resources), the next category down from Endangered. The Jamaican Boa (*Epicrates subflavus*) is also listed as Vulnerable.

Superfamily Henophidia
Family Bolyeridae
Common name Round Island boas
Distinguishing features The family Bolyeridae was originally considered a subfamily of the Boidae but was reclassified as a separate family in 1982. Bolyerid snakes are unique among vertebrates in having both of their maxilla (the bones of the upper jaw) split into two separate elements. There were originally two species in this family. The second, the Round Island Burrowing Boa (*Bolyeria multocarinata*), has not been seen alive since 1975 and is presumed extinct.
Number of species 1
Largest species The Round Island Keel-scaled Boa (*Casarea dussumieri*) is the only living bolyerid and grows up to 4ft 6in (138cm) long.

Smallest species As the only living bolyerid, the Round Island Keel-scaled Boa is also the smallest member of its family.
Distribution Round Island, a tiny islet of just 0.65 square miles (1.69km^2) in the Indian Ocean, 14 miles (22.5km) north of Mauritius.
Principal habitats The natural habitat of the Round Island Keel-scaled Boa was tropical hardwood forest and palm savannah. However, most of this habitat was destroyed following the introduction of rabbits and goats to the island. The snake now lives mainly in the remaining degraded areas of palm savannah and shrub layer vegetation.
Principal prey The Round Island Keel-scaled Boa lives almost exclusively on a diet of lizards, some of which are also endangered and found only on Round Island.
Most endangered species The Round Island Keel-scaled Boa is listed as Critically Endangered by the IUCN and is one of the world's rarest snakes. There are thought to be no more than 1000 individuals left in the wild. A captive breeding program has been set up to ensure the future of the species.

Superfamily Henophidia
Family Cylindrophiidae
Common name Asian pipe snakes
Distinguishing features Asian pipe snakes have stout bodies, blunt heads and short tails. Their smooth scales give them a shiny appearance and all ten species have black and white checkered patterns on their bellies. When threatened, Asian pipe snakes curl up and stick out their tail from the coils as if it was the head. One species, Linne's Earth Snake (*Cylindrophis maculatus*), has a flattened tail which it raises to mimic the head and hood of a cobra. Asian pipe snakes give birth to relatively large, live young, mothers bearing between two and five babies, each between a third and half her body length. The Asian pipe snakes were originally considered to belong to the family Aniliidae, but they were given their own family in 1982.
Number of species 10
Largest species The Red-tailed Pipe Snake (*Cylindrophis ruffus*) from Thailand and Peninsular Malaysia is believed to be the largest member of this family. It grows to a maximum length of around 2ft 11in (90cm).
Smallest species Unknown
Distribution All these snakes are found in South-East Asia, from Sri Lanka, through the Malay Peninsula to the islands of Indonesia.
Principal habitats Most Asian pipe snakes live in tropical forest habitats. Although they are sometimes seen on the surface, these species hunt by burrowing through the leaf litter and soft forest soil. The Red-tailed Pipe Snake inhabits paddy fields and swamps.
Principal prey Most Asian pipe snakes feed on earthworms and small vertebrates they find in the leaf litter. The Red-tailed Pipe Snake, however, hunts larger prey, including other snakes and eels.
Most endangered species Unknown

Superfamily Henophidia
Family Loxocemidae
Common name Mexican Burrowing Snake
Distinguishing features The family Loxocemidae is another family containing just one species, the Mexican Burrowing Snake (*Loxocemus bicolor*). This snake has some features in common with the boas but it lays eggs rather than giving birth to live young. It has large scales on its head but much smaller scales on its body. The mouth is small and the snout points upward.
Number of species 1
Largest species The Mexican Burrowing Snake is the only loxocemid snake and reaches a maximum length of around 5ft (1.53m) but most adults are smaller, averaging 3ft 3in (1m) long.
Smallest species As the only loxocemid snake, the Mexican Burrowing Snake is also the smallest member of its family.
Distribution The Mexican Burrowing Snake occurs from south-western Mexico to northern Costa Rica.
Principal habitats This snake inhabits tropical forests, both moist and dry. It also sometimes forages on coastal beaches. The Mexican Burrowing Snake hunts on the surface at night but spends the day hidden, burrowed into the soil or leaf litter.
Principal prey This snake hunts a wide range of small prey, including lizards and rodents. It has also been known to feed on the eggs of iguanas and both the eggs and hatchling young of sea turtles.
Most endangered species The Mexican Burrowing Snake is not considered to be threatened.

Superfamily Henophidia
Family Pythonidae
Common name Pythons
Distinguishing features Pythons, like boas, are primitive snakes possessing two lungs instead of the usual one. All the members of this family lay eggs. Pythons are non-venomous snakes that kill their prey by constriction. Like boas, they have heat-sensitive pits which enable them to 'see' prey in the dark. In boas, these pits are located between the scales that line the upper lip. In pythons, the pits are located at the centers of these scales.
Number of species 36
Largest species Although not as massive as the Green Anaconda (*Eunectes murinus*), the Reticulated Python (*Python reticulatus*) is the world's longest snake, at least as far as official records go. The longest individual ever measured was a full 32ft 10in (10m) from nose to tail.
Smallest species The Anthill or Pygmy Python (*Antaresia perthensis*) from Australia is the smallest member of this family, measuring up to 2ft 3in (70cm) long.
Distribution Pythons are found in Africa, Asia, and Australia. Most live in tropical or subtropical regions.
Principal habitats Pythons live in a wide range of habitats, from rainforests and wetlands to grasslands and deserts.

Principal prey Pythons feed mainly on vertebrates, from rodents and lizards to many larger than themselves, including deer.
Most endangered species Ramsay's Python (*Aspidites ramsayi*) which is found in Australia.

Superfamily Henophidia
Family Tropidophiidae
Common name Dwarf boas
Distinguishing features Dwarf boas lie between true boas and colubrid snakes in many aspects of their anatomy. Like boas, they have the vestiges of a pelvis and hind limbs – in male dwarf boas the latter protrude through the scales as spurs. Their lungs, however, are more like those of colubrids. The left lung is either greatly reduced in size or completely absent. Some dwarf boas lay eggs but the majority of species give birth to live young.
Number of species 25
Largest species The Cuban Wood Snake (*Tropidophis melanurus*) is by far the largest of the dwarf boas, growing up to 3ft 6in (106cm) long.
Smallest species The Cuban Dusky Dwarf Boa (*Tropidophis fuscus*) is the smallest member of this family, with a maximum length of around 1ft (30cm).
Distribution Most dwarf boa species are found in the Caribbean and Central and South America. The greatest variety occurs on the island of Cuba, where the absence of most other snakes has allowed the dwarf boas to diversify. Two species placed in this family at the time of writing, the spinejaw snakes, come from Malaysia, although it seems likely that they might be given their own family at some point in the future.
Principal habitats Dwarf boas are most common in forests and woodland, although a few species may also be found in rocky areas.
Principal prey The majority of dwarf boas hunt and feed on lizards and amphibians, being too small to tackle most mammals or birds.
Most endangered species Unknown. No members of this family are listed as Threatened or Endangered by the IUCN.

Superfamily Henophidia
Family Uropeltidae
Common name Shieldtail snakes
Distinguishing features The common name of these snakes refers to their most obvious distinguishing feature, a large keratinous shield which they have at the tip of the tail. Shieldtail snakes are burrowers and have smooth, shiny bodies. Most species have almost conical heads with pointed snouts. Unlike many other burrowing snakes, they have teeth in both their upper and lower jaws. All shieldtail snakes give birth to live young.
Number of species 47
Largest species Schneider's Earth Snake (*Rhinophis oxyrhynchus*), from south-western India, is thought to be the largest member of this family. It grows to a maximum length of 1ft 10in (57cm).
Smallest species Unknown
Distribution Shieldtail snakes are found only in southern India and Sri Lanka.

Principal habitats Shieldtail snakes spend most of their time in the soil.

Principal prey Earthworms make up the bulk of the diet of most species. Other burrowing invertebrates, such as insect larvae, are also eaten.

Most endangered species Unknown

Superfamily Henophidia

Family Xenopeltidae

Common name Sunbeam snakes

Distinguishing features The little known sunbeam snakes are burrowers and like other burrowing snakes have very smooth scales. The scales of sunbeam snakes, however, have another, unusual quality – when sunlight hits them they act like prisms, splitting the light and making their owners appear to glisten with all the colors of the rainbow. It is this feature that gives these otherwise unremarkable looking, slightly flattened burrowing snakes their name.

Number of species 2

Largest species The Common Sunbeam Snake (*Xenopeltis unicolor*) may grow to lengths of 3ft 3in (1m) or more.

Smallest species The Hainan Sunbeam Snake (*Xenopeltis hainanensis*) is known to reach 2ft 1in (64cm) long.

Distribution Sunbeam snakes occur throughout South-East Asia, from Myanmar (Burma) and the Andaman and Nicobar Islands through Thailand, Laos, Cambodia, Vietnam, southern China, Malaysia, and parts of Indonesia to the Philippines.

Principal habitats Sunbeam snakes are common on agricultural land and the edges of woodland. It is thought that they may also be common in forests but data on them outside settled areas is sparse.

Principal prey Burrowing into the soil or leaf litter to hide by day, sunbeam snakes emerge to hunt on the surface at night. Their prey includes a wide variety of small vertebrates, from frogs, lizards, and other snakes to rodents and birds.

Most endangered species Neither species is considered to be endangered.

Superfamily Typhlopoidea

Family Anomalepididae

Common name Early blind snakes

Distinguishing features These small, smooth-bodied snakes look a lot like other blind snakes. However, experts can tell them apart by subtle differences in their dentition and the patterns made by their scales. Some early blind snakes have teeth on both the upper and lower jaws, rather than on just one or the other of these. Early blind snakes have very small eyes that are sometimes almost completely covered by scales. Their mouths are small and their bodies slender and cylindrical, all adaptations to a life of burrowing.

Number of species 16

Largest species Unknown. Four species (*Liotyphlops anops, L. beui, L. schubarti* and *L. ternetzii*) may exceed lengths of 1ft (30cm) but most are considerably smaller.

Smallest species Unknown

Distribution This family is confined to southern Central America and northern and central eastern South America.

Principal habitats These snakes live in the soil, usually in the vicinity of ant or termite nests. They tend to be found near the surface, although one specimen was recovered from a depth of 1ft 8in (50cm) below the ground.

Principal prey Although the feeding habits of some early blind snakes have not been studied, those that have feed almost entirely on ants and termites.

Most endangered species Although no early blind snakes are listed by the IUCN as Threatened or Endangered, these snakes are extremely poorly studied. Some are known by just a single specimen. As a result, the abundance of most early blind snakes remains unclear.

Superfamily Typhlopoidea

Family Leptotyphlopidae

Common name Slender blind snakes

Distinguishing features Slender blind snakes have tiny, cylindrical bodies covered with close-fitting, shiny scales. They are distinguished from other blind snakes in their size and the fact that they have no teeth at all in their lower jaw. Slender blind snakes include most of the species commonly called thread snakes or worm snakes and many of them are little bigger than earthworms. Many have pink or brown scales, making them look so much like earthworms that they could easily be confused for them at first glance.

Number of species Approximately 100

Largest species Two species share this title, the Western Thread Snake (*Leptotyphlops occidentalis*) and the Espírito Santo Blind Snake (*Leptotyphlops salgueiroi*), both of which come from Brazil and regularly grow to more than 1ft (30cm) long.

Smallest species The Lesser Antillean Threadsnake (*Leptotyphlops bilineata*) is the world's smallest snake. It grows to a maximum length of 4in (10.8cm) and has a body no wider than a matchstick. The Lesser Antillean Threadsnake lives on the islands of Martinique, Barbados, and St. Lucia in the Caribbean.

Distribution Most slender blind snakes live in tropical Africa and Central and South America. Two species range into the south-western USA and another two occur in Pakistan and India.

Principal habitats All of these snakes live in the soil or leaf litter, usually in the vicinity of ant or termite nests.

Principal prey Ants and termites. These snakes are so small that they do not even swallow their prey whole, instead breaking through the tough exoskeleton and sucking out the insides.

Most endangered species Unknown

Superfamily Typhlopoidea

Family Typhlopidae

Common name Blind snakes

Distinguishing features To look at, these snakes appear very similar to the other blind snakes. Like them, they lack the large belly scales found in most other snakes. However, they differ from other blind snakes in having a toothless lower jaw composed entirely of a single compound bone. The upper jaw bears several teeth.

Number of species Approximately 240

Largest species Schlegel's Giant Blind Snake (*Rhinotyphlops schlegelii schlegelii*) is the largest member of this family, growing up to 3ft (95cm) long.

Smallest species Unknown

Distribution There are members of this family on every continent apart from Antarctica, including one species in Europe (*Typhlops vermicularis*) and two in North America (*T. pusillus* and *T. lumbricalis*, both from Florida).

Principal habitats These snakes are found in the soil in a wide range of habitats, but almost always near to or inside the nests of ants or termites.

Principal prey As with other blind snakes, all of the members of this family are formicophagous, that is to say they feed on a diet of termites and ants, particularly their eggs and larvae.

Most endangered species The Mona Island Blind Snake (*Typhlops monensis*) is listed as Endangered by the IUCN and the Christmas Island Blind Snake (*Ramphotyphlops exocoeti*) as Vulnerable. There may be other species at risk of extinction but because so many of them are very little studied their status cannot be established.

Superfamily Xenophidia

Family Acrochordidae

Common name Wart snakes

Distinguishing features The most obvious difference between wart snakes and other snakes is their skin. Wart snakes have skin that appears to be a few sizes too big for them, being loose, baggy, and crumpled like an oversized sweater. They also have unusual scales, which project from the skin like tiny pyramids and give it a rough texture, hence their other common name, the file snakes. Wart snakes differ in other ways too, lacking the broad belly scales found on most other snakes and having their eyes positioned on the top rather than the sides of their heads.

Number of species 3

Largest species The Elephant Trunk Snake or Java File Snake (*Acrochordus javanicus*) holds this record, growing to more than 6ft 6in (2m) long.

Smallest species The Little File Snake (*Acrochordus granulatus*), as its name suggests, is the smallest member of this family. It grows to a maximum length of around 3ft 3in (1m).

Distribution Wart snakes are found in India, South-East Asia, and Australia.

Principal habitats All three species are aquatic. The Little File Snake is mainly marine, inhabiting coastal waters and mangrove swamps, but also

enters freshwater habitats. The other two species live in freshwater lagoons, rivers and streams.

Principal prey All wart snakes feed almost exclusively on fish.

Most endangered species None of these snakes is considered to be threatened.

Superfamily Xenophidia

Family Atractaspididae

Common name Burrowing asps

Distinguishing features These snakes resemble colubrid snakes in most respects. However, the members of the best known genus, Atractaspis, the stiletto snakes, differ markedly in their dentition. Stiletto snakes have a pair of long, hollow fangs at the fronts of their mouths which can be erected like those of vipers. The way in which they are moved into position, however, differs. Rather than being simply pulled forward from their resting position on the roof of the mouth, they swing out sideways, allowing the snakes to strike with their mouths still almost closed, by swiping their heads sideways. Other members of this family include the harlequin snakes, which have fixed front fangs like cobras.

Number of species 62

Largest species Unknown. None of these snakes reach much more than 3ft 3in (1m) long.

Smallest species Unknown

Distribution Most members of this family live in sub-Saharan Africa. Two species have ranges that extend into Israel and Jordan.

Principal habitats Some of these snakes dig through the soil and leaf litter in search of prey, while others live and hunt in the burrows of other animals. They are found in a variety of habitats, ranging from forest and savannah, to semi-desert.

Principal prey Different species specialize in hunting different prey. Animals eaten range from earthworms and giant centipedes to rodents, lizards and other snakes.

Most endangered species None of the burrowing asps are considered to be threatened.

Superfamily Xenophidia

Family Colubridae

Common name Colubrid snakes

Distinguishing features This is by far the largest snake family and contains a huge variety of snakes. That said, all colubrids have certain features in common. All have a single lung or two lungs with the left one extremely reduced and lack any vestiges of a pelvis or hind limbs (unlike all blind snakes, boas and pythons). While a few colubrid species are venomous, none of these has fangs at the front of its mouth – indeed all of the back-fanged venomous snakes are colubrids.

Number of species Approximately 1700

Largest species Unknown. Several species exceed 8ft (2.5m) long.

Smallest species Unknown.

Distribution There are members of this family on every continent apart from Australia and Antarctica. They range from near the edge of the Arctic Circle to the Equator.

Principal habitats Colubrid snakes are found in all the habitats in which other snakes occur, apart from the sea.

Principal prey Most colubrids hunt relatively small prey. Animals eaten range from invertebrates such as slugs to rodents, lizards, fish, amphibians, and other snakes. Some colubrids specialize in eating eggs.

Most endangered species Five members of this family are listed as Critically Endangered by the IUCN. They are the Antiguan Racer (*Alsophis antiguae*), the Black Racer (*Alsophis ater*) from Jamaica, the Saint Vincent Blacksnake (*Chironius vincenti*), the Martinique Groundsnake (*Liophis cursor*), and Kikuzato's Brook Snake (*Opisthotropis kikuzatoi*) from Japan. Many other species are listed in the slightly lower risk categories of Endangered and Vulnerable.

Superfamily Xenophidia
Family Elapidae
Common name Cobras, coral snakes and kraits
Distinguishing features All of the members of this family are venomous. They are characterized by their fixed front fangs, which are permanently erect and fit into slots in the floor of the mouth. In most other respects elapids are similar to colubrid snakes, having either a single lung or two lungs with the left one being greatly reduced and lacking any vestiges of a pelvis. Elapids also lack the heat-detecting pits found in boas, pythons and many vipers.
Number of species Approximately 300
Largest species The King Cobra (*Ophiophagus hannah*) is the largest member of this family. It grows up to 18ft 8in (5.7m) long.
Smallest species Unknown
Distribution Elapids are found in every continent apart from Europe and Antarctica. However, they are confined mainly to tropical and subtropical regions.
Principal habitats Some elapids are burrowers, while some, such as the mambas and tree cobras spend a lot of their time in the branches. Most species, however, hunt on the ground. They live in a variety of habitats, from rainforests to grasslands and deserts.
Principal prey These snakes hunt vertebrate prey, ranging from fish, amphibians and other reptiles to small mammals and birds.
Most endangered species Seven elapids are listed as Vulnerable by the IUCN. The two thought to be at greatest risk are Dunmall's Snake (*Furina dunmalli*) and the Ornamental Snake (*Denisonia maculata*), both from Australia.

Superfamily Xenophidia
Family Hydrophiidae
Common name Sea snakes
Distinguishing features Sea snakes have many features in common with elapid snakes and for a long time they were both grouped into the same family by scientists. The most obvious difference between the two groups is their lifestyle: sea snakes live in the ocean whereas elapids live on land or in freshwater habitats. Like elapids, sea snakes produce venom which they inject through fixed fangs, positioned at the front of the mouth. Unlike elapids, sea snakes have tails that are vertically flattened to act as paddles and help propel them through the water.
Number of species Approximately 50
Largest species The longest sea snake is the Yellow Sea Snake (*Hydrophis spiralis*), which lives in the northern Indian Ocean. It grows up to 9ft (2.75m) long.
Smallest species Unknown
Distribution Sea snakes are confined to the world's tropical seas. They are most common in the Indian and Pacific Oceans.
Principal habitats Most sea snakes live in coastal waters, where there is the greatest abundance of fish. Many are common around coral reefs, while some enter mangrove swamps and estuaries to hunt.
Principal prey Fish
Most endangered species Only one species of seas snake is listed as Vulnerable by the IUCN, Crocker's Sea Snake (*Laticauda crockeri*), which is found in the waters around the Solomon Islands.

Superfamily Xenophidia
Family Viperidae
Common name Vipers
Distinguishing features Vipers are probably the best known of all snakes. They have broad, roughly triangular heads and produce venom, which they inject using long, hinged fangs at the fronts of their mouths. These fangs are only raised when the snake is about to strike. Normally they are folded back against the roof of the mouth. Many vipers have pits on their heads which enable them to detect the body heat of their prey.
Number of species 224
Largest species The largest viper is the Eastern Diamondback Rattlesnake (*Crotalus adamanteus*) from North America. It may weigh as much as 34lb (15kg) and can grow to more than 6ft 6in (2m) long.
Smallest species The Spotted Dwarf Adder (*Bitis schneideri*) from Namibia is the world's smallest viper. It grows to a maximum length of just 11in (28cm).
Distribution Vipers are found in all the world's continents apart from Australia and Antarctica. They range from just south of the Arctic Circle to the Equator.
Principal habitats Vipers are found in most terrestrial habitats, from mountains and boreal forests to deserts.
Principal prey All vipers hunt and kill other vertebrate animals. Their prey ranges from rodents and lizards to small forest antelopes.
Most endangered species Six vipers are listed as Critically Endangered by the IUCN. They are the Aruba Island Rattlesnake (*Crotalus unicolor*), the Golden Lancehead (*Bothrops insularis*) and the Alcatrazes Lancehead (*Bothrops alcatraz*), both from Brazil, the Mount Bulgar Viper (*Vipera bulgardaghica*) from Turkey, and the sand vipers *Vipera darevskii* and *Vipera pontica* from Turkey, Armenia, and Georgia.

INDEX

Acrochordidae 16, 94

anaconda 30,32, 40, 64, 67, 70, 88, 91

Aniliidae 90, 91

Anomalepididae 93

Anomochilus 90

arboreal snakes 22, 24, 32, 33, 36, 40, 46, 57, 64, 67, 70, 73, 80, 83, 91, 95

Atractaspididae 94

basking 8, 67, 69, 79

behavior 7, 8, 20-49, 56, 66, 76

blind snakes 14, 16, 40, 80, 90, 93, 94

boa 13, 14, 16, 22, 24, 32, 51, 64, 67, 70, 72, 80, 89, 91, 92, 94, 95

Boidae 14, 91

Bolyeridae 90

breeding 21, 44-49, 64, 66, 70, 91

burrowing snake 14, 16, 29, 42, 42, 70, 79, 90-95

camouflage 11, 13, 33, 36, 39, 40, 67

cobra 14, 16, 24, 42, 44, 51, 52, 55, 56, 57, 76, 88, 91, 94, 95

Colubridae 14, 51, 76, 80, 94

Colubrid snake 14, 16, 39, 76, 79, 80, 92, 94, 95

coral snake 40, 52, 79, 90, 95

Cylindrophiidae 91

defense 30, 40, 52, 55, 56, 69, 76

eggs (snake) 44-49, 70, 90-95

egg-eating snakes 8, 34, 36, 80, 92, 94

Elapidae 14, 76, 95

endangered 67, 70, 80, 90-95

fangs 10, 14, 16, 39, 55, 56, 76, 88, 94, 95

feeding 14, 34-43, 55, 56, 64, 70, 76, 77, 78, 79, 80, 89, 90-95

fish-eating 16, 36, 56, 57, 76, 94, 95

habitat 27, 39, 64, 67, 70, 79, 87, 90-95

heaviest snakes 55, 88

Henophidia 14, 90-93

hibernation 8, 22, 44, 49, 79

Hydrophiidae 16, 95

jaws 8, 10, 14, 16, 24, 34, 36, 91, 92, 93, 94

Leptotyphlopidae 93

live young 46, 49, 70, 79, 90, 91, 92, 93, 94

locomotion 13, 29, 30, 32

longest snake

Loxocemidae 92

mamba 49, 55, 88, 95

movement 10, 22-33, 79, 80 – *see also locomotion*

pipe snake 90, 91

predators 7, 13, 22, 32, 34-43, 44, 46, 48, 64, 66, 69, 70, 76, 78, 79

prey 8, 10, 13, 14, 21, 22-33, 34-43, 48, 52-63, 64-75, 76-85, 89, 90-95

python 10, 13, 14, 16, 22, 24, 30, 32, 40, 42, 38, 39, 44, 46, 51, 64–75, 88, 89, 91, 92, 95

Pythonidae 14, 92

rattlesnake 10, 22, 24, 27, 29, 40, 42, 44, 46, 49, 55, 60, 80, 89, 95

sea snake 14, 16, 30, 46, 51, 52, 56, 57, 89, 94, 95

senses 22-33, 36, 67, 80, 89, 92

sidewinding 29

skeleton 10, 13, 30, 88, 90, 91

smallest snake 40, 55, 80, 88, 90-95

snake bite 8, 40, 52, 55, 56, 60, 88

snake skin 8, 13, 16, 44, 67, 70, 94

thread snakes 40, 80, 93

tree-climbing snakes – *see arboreal snakes*

Tropidophiidae 92

Typhlopidae 93

Uropeltidae 92

venomous 13, 14, 16, 39, 40, 42, 51, 52-63, 76, 79, 80, 88, 89, 92, 94, 95

viper 8, 10, 14, 22, 24, 26, 36, 39, 51, 52, 55, 56, 57, 60, 76, 88, 89, 94, 95

Viperidae 14, 95

wart snake 16, 94

Xenopeltidae 93

Xenophidia 14, 94, 95

young snakes 44-49, 67

Picture Credits

© **Corbis:**
Theo Allofs 70-71, 84-85; Anthony Bannister/Gallo Images 49 (center); Brandon D. Cole 30 (left); W. Perry Conway 39 (above right), 60-61 (below); Nigel J. Dennis/Gallo Images 57 (left); DK Limited 57 (below right); Michael & Patricia Fogden 16 (below), 28, 36 (center), 37 (below); Victor Fraile/Reuters 10 (left); Shai Ginott 37 (above); Steve Kaufman 49 (above), 54; Herbert Kehrer/ zefa 22; Stefan Kiefer/dpa 66; Robert Marien 77; Chris Mattison/Frank Lane Picture Agency 39 (below left), 47, 82-83; Joe McDonald 10-11, 32 (above), 55 (above), 67 (above), 80, 74 75; Mary Ann McDonald 58-59; Arthur Morris 41; Werner H. Mueller/zefa 9; Chris Newton/Frank Lane

Picture Agency 40; David A. Northcott 18-19, 26-27, 35, 62-63, 65, 68-69, 48; Rod Patterson/ Gallo Images 49 (below); 56 (above); Josh Westrich/zefa 38.

© **istockphoto.com:**
Terry J Alcorn 25; Jeffrey Anderson 46 (above); Anzeletti 88 (right); Joseph Brewster 67 (below); Daniel Brunner 29; Henry Chaplin 64; Michael Chen 21 (right); Dan Danny 56 (below); Demonoid 39 (above left); Philip Dyer 79 (below); Daniel Eitzen 72-73; eROMAZe 15; Steffen Foerster 34; Andrea Gingerich 11, 88 (left); George Hoeylaerts 36 (below); Falk Kienas 8 (left); Sean Martin 46 (center); Neal McClimon 78 (below); Nathan Menifee 89 (above); Juan Monino 55 (below); Photobar 52; John Pitcher 24 (below); Heiko Potthoff 86-87; Lawrence Sawyer 79 (above); Dan Schmitt 17, 57

(above right); Lara Seregni 33 (above); Natalia Sinjushina & Evgeniy Meyke 51; Wolfgang Staib 76; Jeryl Tan 50-51; Brad Thompson 24 (above); Jim Travis 14; Nicola Vernizzi 1; Alice Weniger 46 (below); Paul Wolf 60-61 (above); Roy van Zijl 36 (above).

© **shutterstock.com:**
Lynsey Allan 81; Sascha Burkard 12; CoverStock 78 (above); EcoPrint 23, 54, 90; Sebastian Gauthier 7 (right); Robert Adrian Hillman 32 (below); Michael Ledray 45; Bruce MacQueen 44; Milos Markovic 2-3; Claus Mikosch 13 (below); Kim Murrell 33 (below); Anita Patterson Peppers 87 (right); Brad Phillips 42-43; Matasa Constantin Radu 13 (above); Elan Sablich 20-21; Brenda Ariene Smith 89 (below); Brad Thompson 6-7; Gary Unwin 30-31; Tim Zurowski 16 (above).

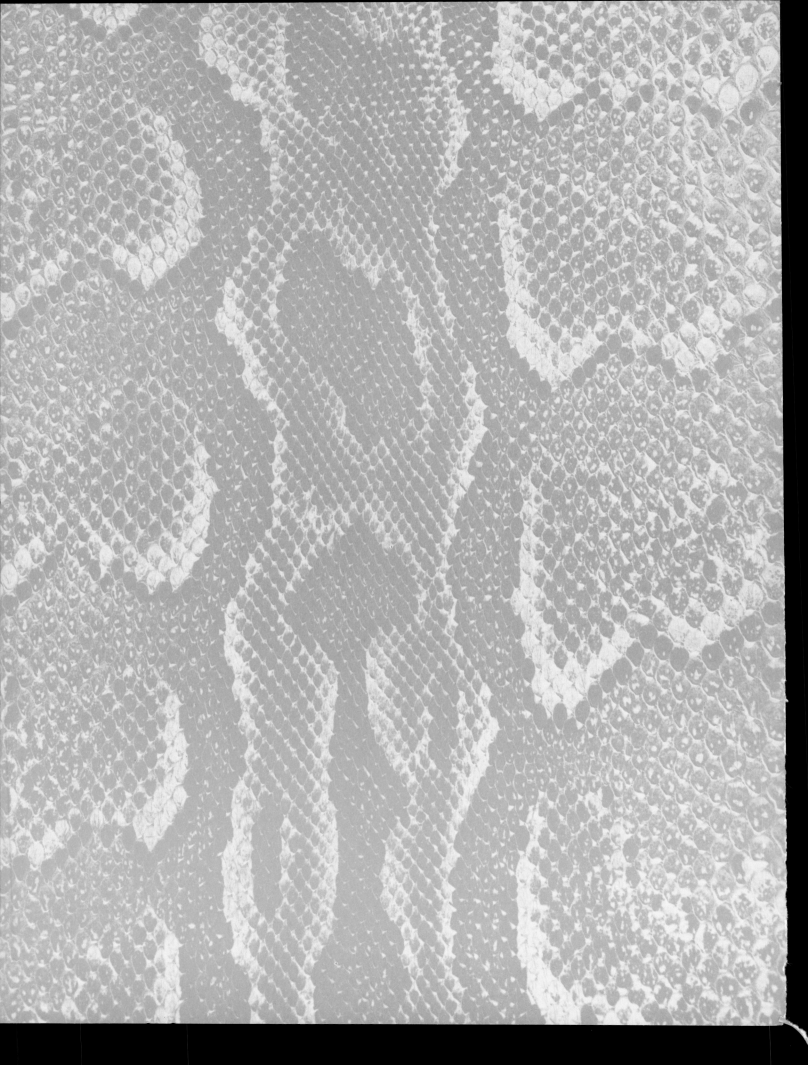